OSPREY AIRCRAFT OF THE ACES 120

P-38 LIGHTNING ACES 1942-43

SERIES EDITOR: TONY HOLMES

OSPREY AIRCRAFT OF THE ACES 120

P-38 LIGHTNING ACES 1942-43

John Stanaway

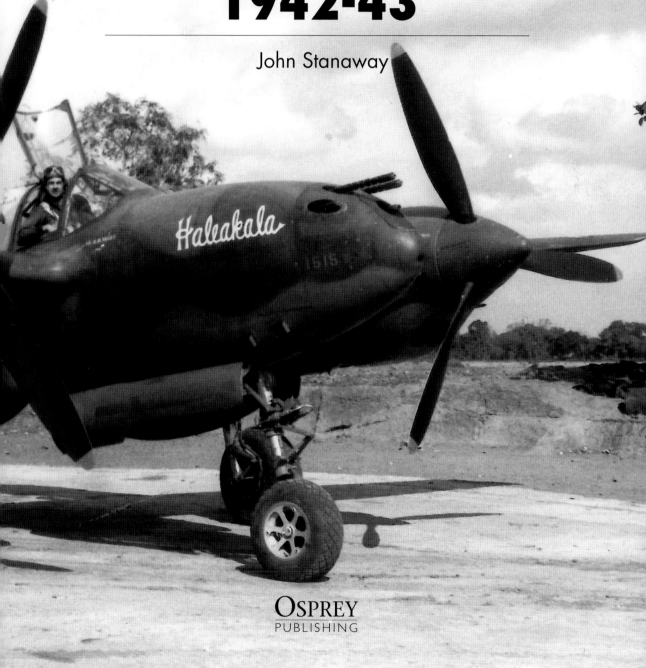

OSPREY
PUBLISHING

Front Cover
On 29 October 1943, future ace 1Lt John 'Jump' O'Neill of the 9th FS/49th FG claimed his final two victories in P-38G-15 43-2204 *Beautiful Lass*. On that day he was element leader within Capt Bill Haney's B-24 bomber escort formation. Capt Haney, flying as 'Flying Knight' mission leader, had led his P-38s to northern New Britain, where the Liberator strike force paraded over Cape Gazelle before turning west-northwest onto their bomb line. The B-24s were targeting enemy shipping anchored in Simpson Harbour. Haney's three flights were stacked between 20,000 ft and 22,000 ft in the clear sky, and they quickly saw the rising swarm of fighters arching in from the north. In a near perfect interception, all but 2Lt Glade Hill dropped their external tanks and plunged into the enemy formation in one thundering pass.

Blue element wingman Hill separated from his squadronmates momentarily and rocked his P-38 to loosen his stuck belly tanks, but Haney did not wait for him. With element leader 1Lt John O'Neill and wingman 2Lt John McLean following close by, Haney peeled off and headed for the Japanese fighters as Hill finally jettisoned his tanks, only to find that his starboard supercharger would not run at full power. Although Hill was several seconds to the rear, all four Blue elements hit the Imperial Japanese Naval Air Force Zero-sen fighters at 18,000 ft and made two firing passes in their 400 mph spiralling descent down to the treetops. Just above the jungle, near Vunakanau airfield (called Rabaul West by the Japanese), 'Jump' O'Neill gunned down kills numbers seven and eight for the last two victories of his tour (*Cover artwork by Mark Postlethwaite*)

First published in Great Britain in 2014 by Osprey Publishing
PO Box 883, Oxford, OX1 9PL, UK
PO Box 3985, New York, NY 10185-3985, USA

E-mail: info@ospreypublishing.com

Osprey Publishing is part of the Osprey Group

A CIP catalogue record for this book is available from the British Library

ISBN: 978 1 78200 332 8
PDF e-book ISBN: 978 1 78200 333 5
e-Pub ISBN: 978 1 78200 334 2

Edited by Bruce Hales-Dutton and Tony Holmes
Cover Artwork by Mark Postlethwaite
Aircraft Profiles by Chris Davey
Index by Sandra Shotter
Originated by PDQ Digital Media Solutions, UK
Printed in China through Asia Pacific Offset Limited

14 15 16 17 18   10 9 8 7 6 5 4 3 2 1

Osprey Publishing is supporting the Woodland Trust, the UK's leading woodland conservation charity, by funding the dedication of trees.

www.ospreypublishing.com

Acknowledgements
Old friends once again came to the author's aid during the compilation of this book, with photographs supplied by Steve Blake, Mike Bates, Jack Cook and Jim Lansdale. In addition, newer friends like Jon Bernstein, Jean Barbaud, Bonnie Hancock, Peter Randall and Luke Ruffato have helped illuminate Mediterranean, Pacific and CBI details. I should also mention the written works of Christopher Shores, Bill Hess and Frank Olynyk, to which I heavily referred in resolving many historic questions about opposing sides in various engagements.

CONTENTS

INTRODUCTION

The later P-38 Lightning models were honed to the finest edge that Lockheed could produce. In fact, the ultimate fighting example (the P-38J-25) was both fast enough and manoeuvrable enough to match the latest piston-engined fighters of the Luftwaffe up to an altitude of approximately 30,000 ft. With aileron boost, compressibility-dampening flaps and Allison V-1710-111 and -113 engines able to produce 1475 hp at 30,000 ft, the J-25 was the fastest of the production series with a top speed exceeding 420 mph. The J-25 could – according to Lockheed – dive with anything short of the Me 163 rocket fighter. It could climb with any conventional propeller-driven aircraft of the era and could even stay with the superbly manoeuvrable Mitsubishi A6M Zero throughout much of its turning radius.

Unfortunately, the J-25 was not available until mid 1944, when 105 examples arrived in the European Theatre of Operations (ETO) and were assigned in their entirety to the tactical Ninth Air Force. The essentially similar L-model soon followed the J-25 off the Lockheed assembly line from July 1944. For the rest of the war in the ETO and, to a lesser extent, in other theatres of war involving the USAAF, the P-38 was increasingly used as a tactical fighter due to its growing obsolescence as an interceptor.

Up until the end of 1943, however, the Lightning earned a reputation as the USAAF's premier fighter. Indeed, by January 1944 its exploits in the Pacific had made the P-38 the most sought-after fighter in the USAAF arsenal. Although produced in smaller numbers than any other major American fighter of World War 2, every theatre commander wanted the P-38 because of its range, versatility and altitude performance.

The first models to see combat (E to H) were heavily criticised for their lack of modern automation, basic pilot comfort and poor power-to-weight ratio at higher altitudes. Yet despite their shortcomings these early P-38s were delivered into the eager hands of American pilots who took to the skies over every front to which US forces were committed. They also wrote a sterling record for the unconventional fighter. Approximately 100 of an eventual total of some 175 P-38 aces scored the prerequisite five victories to qualify as aces in the early E- to H-models. Indeed, most of the top aces, including Bong, McGuire, Sloan and Leverette, had scored at least half of their total victories by the end of 1943.

Using the comments of these aces themselves, as well as documents detailing the tactics used by various USAAF fighter units, this narrative will show how these early P-38s not only survived in skies dominated by deadly Axis fighters, but to a large degree also dominated the tactical and strategic situations they found themselves embroiled in.

LOCKHEED'S HOT ROD

The P-38 Lightning was initially issued to the USAAF's 1st Fighter Group (FG) in April 1941. Later that same year other groups, including the 14th and 82nd FGs, acquired their Lightnings (mostly E-models) and prepared for operations. The 20th and 55th FGs received P-38s during the second half of 1942. By January 1943 these units, plus the 78th FG (which lost its Lightnings to the Twelfth Air Force once in England), would either be on their way to Europe or preparing to deploy to the ETO.

The first deployment of Lightnings to an operational theatre, however, came in mid-1942 in response to the Japanese diversionary invasion of the Aleutian Islands in the northern Pacific. P-38Es of the 343rd FG and the 28th Composite Group were rushed to Alaskan bases to counter expected Japanese incursions. By then the 8th Photographic Squadron's F-4 Lightnings had already been deployed to Australia.

The P-38 had been designed to meet a requirement for a heavily armed, fast-climbing bomber interceptor to guard US territory against possible attack. Reports from southeast Asia suggesting that long-range bombers could threaten the United States from land bases or aircraft carriers worried American planners. This concern was to lead to one of the most remarkable fighter aircraft of the period. What the design team at Lockheed under Clarence 'Kelly' Johnson and Hall Hibbard managed to create was a twin-engined, fast-climbing, heavily armed fighter that also had a phenomenal load-carrying capacity. The counter-rotating propellers made the P-38 extremely manoeuvrable at various altitudes and the multi-engine configuration gave it great range for a fighter of its era.

Lockheed stressed to the USAAF and to new P-38 pilots the importance of climbing away from hostile aircraft as a prime combat tactic. The Lightning could easily out-climb even single-engined fighters in 1942, contradicting the standard evasive tactic of turning away and diving in order to lose a pursuer. In fact, the P-38's superior rate of climb gave pilots an effective tactical manoeuvre throughout the war. German opponents, in particular, respected the Lightning's ability to pursue them after a bounce without the necessary boost achieved from a 'dive-and-zoom' manoeuvre. Many an Axis fighter pilot would look back in astonishment to see the P-38 he had just attacked now closing in on him in a climb.

But the main P-38 attribute feared by Axis crews was its armament. German pilots were warned not to tackle a Lightning head-on if it could be avoided. The fighter's battery of four Browning M2 0.50-in machine guns and single Oldsmobile-manufactured Hispano M1 20 mm cannon was concentrated in the nose to produce a tight circumference of fire not much larger than a basketball. Even in a tight turn all five guns would usually function to produce a weight of fire that could reportedly penetrate the hull of a destroyer.

What Allied pilots liked most about the P-38 was its range. Any target within a radius of about 400 miles was easily reached by the Lightning. Commanders in the North African as well as the Pacific theatres came to rely on the Lockheed fighter for long-range interceptions as well as strafing and bombing missions. Ordnance loads were impressive for the period, sometimes surpassing a ton of explosives. Perhaps it was this ability to fly long distances that also served to give some German and Italian pilots the impression that the P-38 was a vulnerable target. Attacks on ground targets made the Lightning especially vulnerable to enemy fighters diving from superior heights. One feature of the P-38 in combat, however, could deceive enemy pilots.

Like the P-47, the Lightning could spew out gouts of dark smoke when the throttles were opened quickly in an emergency, giving the impression the aircraft was crippled. This may be the reason why Luftwaffe aces Kurt Bühligen and Franz Schiess stated that the P-38 was the easiest Allied fighter to down in the North African theatre. Indeed, Schiess claimed to have destroyed an astonishing 17 Lightnings prior to falling victim to one himself. Bühligen was credited with at least 13 P-38 kills.

FIRST VICTORIES

Although built as a fighter, the first P-38 model to see combat was the unarmed F-4 photo-reconnaissance variant. These specialist aircraft were assigned to the newly established 8th Photo Reconnaissance Squadron (PRS), led by 1Lt Karl L 'Pop' Polifka. Placed in command of the unit upon its formation on 1 February 1942, the ex-lumberjack had earned his US Army Air Corps wings in the late 1930s. Descended from Russian-Czech immigrants, Polifka had inherited a solid hatred for the Axis mentality from his parents.

War emergency conditions in the Pacific meant that the 8th PRS was urgently needed in-theatre, so Polifka boarded the SS *President Coolidge* on 19 March 1942 with the squadron's A Flight – its B and C Flights would follow in due course. In the meantime, Polifka would fly the four F-4s with a few officers and enlisted men from Townsville, Queensland, until July 1942. For some of the time he found himself operating virtually single-handedly as three of the four F-4s were grounded due to a lack of spare parts until the threat posed by the Imperial Japanese Navy (IJN) fleet in the southeastern Pacific receded following the Battle of the Coral Sea in early May 1942.

Polifka became a legend when he flew reconnaissance missions over the growing IJN fleet at Rabaul using a B-24 and crew that he had acquired in April. The Japanese undoubtedly heard the high-pitched roar of the P-38's Allison engines for the first time

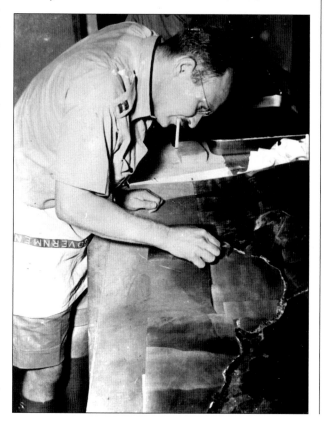

1Lt Karl 'Pop' Polifka studies a recently assembled aerial photo mosaic of the IJN stronghold of Rabaul in early 1942. These photographs were taken during highly dangerous photo-reconnaissance flights made by unarmed F-4 Lightnings of the Townsville-based 8th PRS

WO Schrader, 1Lt Fred Hargesheimer (right) and TSgt Roland Baker pose near the gun bay of Polifka's *Fainting Floozie II* in 1942. Hargesheimer was subsequently shot down on 5 June 1943 by a Ki-45 over New Britain while flying F-5A-10 42-13073. Wandering in the jungle for 31 days, he was eventually found by villagers and hidden from the Japanese for six months until he was handed over to Australian Army commandos

when he had ranged over the gathering fleet in late April and early May. There is little documentation to substantiate the wild stories that emerged from this period, but legend has it that Polifka completed his photo runs over the fleet and then out-ran pursuing Zero-sens with one of his engines shot out! The legend even has the remarkable photo-reconnaissance pilot manoeuvring so skilfully that one of the enemy fighters stalled and crashed into the sea.

There is documentation to support accounts of similar feats by other 8th PRS pilots, notably Capt Alex Guerry over Wewak and Lt Homer Taylor over Rabaul. In the absence of witnesses or photographic proof, these pilots could only be credited with a 'probable' each. In any case, the first undocumented claim for the destruction of an enemy aircraft in World War 2 by a Lightning pilot is attributed to an F-4. Polifka was later to perform yeoman service flying photo-reconnaissance missions in Italy, and he was considered the premier American photo-reconnaissance ace of the war.

The first confirmed P-38 victories were achieved over the Aleutian Islands in August 1942. Japanese forces had made a feint attack towards Alaska before the Midway operation in June, but their coded signals had been broken and American intelligence knew exactly where, and when, the main attack would be made. Reconnaissance for the Japanese offensive on Alaska involved patrols by Kawanishi H6K 'Mavis' flying boats, which in turn prompted the USAAF to rush P-38Es of the 28th Composite Group and 343rd FG north from Washington State to Alaska.

9

Six 'Mavis' flying boats were assigned to the Aleutians following the Japanese occupation of Kiska and Attu in June 1942. IJNAF Capt Sukemitsu Ito intended to lead them in bombing and reconnaissance operations against the Aleutians and western Alaska. However, the campaign got off to a poor start when three of the Kawanishis were lost to the elements. On 4 August Ito was leading the remaining three flying boats towards Umnak Island when an intercepting force of six P-38Es from the 343rd FG's 54th Fighter Squadron (FS), guided by a B-24, intercepted them near Harold's Bay. 1Lts Stanley Long and Kenneth Ambrose, who were part of the third flight (the others had already turned back due to a shortage of fuel), heard a crewman aboard the guiding Liberator call in a speck about ten miles from Great Mountain. Despite encountering alternating sunshine and fog between 3500 ft and 9000 ft, the two P-38 pilots finally spotted two dark dots that stood out against white cloud at 7000 ft.

Ambrose dived on the left-hand 'Mavis' while Long took the one on the right. Ambrose missed with his first burst but Long managed to hit both Japanese aircraft. Long's second pass sent one flying boat spinning into the water off Nazan, while Ambrose's follow-up pass on the other 'Mavis' sent it also into the bay with an engine trailing flame. Ito was subsequently forced to fly the sole remaining H6K back to Japan. The P-38 had achieved its first victories of the war. With the H6Ks gone, only a handful of Nakajima A6M2-N 'Rufe' floatplane fighters (a water-borne variant of the Zero-sen) remained on Kiska, Adak and Attu for bombing and reconnaissance missions.

Another 54th FS pilot had a remarkable record during the early Aleutian fighting. At one time Capt George Laven was unofficially almost an ace in the USAAF's Eleventh Air Force. He had been in the Alaskan theatre

1Lt Stanley Long and Capt George Laven pose with the latter pilot's P-38 in late 1942. Long claimed two kills while serving with the 54th FS, including the first confirmed aerial victory for the Lightning on 4 August 1942 when he downed an H6K 'Mavis' flying boat

Capt George Laven's P-38E 41-2076 bears four victory marks beneath its cockpit. The veteran fighter, assigned to the 54th FS/343rd FG, was photographed at Adak, in the Aleutian Islands, on 29 May 1943

for some time when he shared in the destruction of either a 'Rufe' or an Aichi E13A 'Jake' reconnaissance floatplane (his records indicate an unlikely 'Mavis') moored on the Kiska coast with another 54th FS pilot on 3 September 1942. Eleven days later he claimed to have shot down a biplane over the same distant Kiska area. Laven completed his Aleutian scoring by downing two Zero-sens (possibly 'Rufes') on 13 February 1943. For years later he claimed four aircraft destroyed.

By 1945 Laven was back on operations in the Pacific with the 49th FG, and he claimed a four-engined Kawanishi H8K 'Emily' flying boat for what he considered to be his fifth victory on 26 April. By any account, Laven was the high-scoring P-38 pilot of the Aleutians campaign.

One interesting aspect of Laven's service concerns an assignment to fly his P-38E back to a local maintenance facility in the Aleutians for an overhaul in November 1942. When he found the site inoperable, he simply flew to his old hometown of San Antonio, Texas. After visiting his family, Laven collected his aircraft and flew it back into the war!

GET YAMAMOTO!

When the Allies discovered that the Japanese were building an airstrip on the island of Guadalcanal, in the Solomons archipelago, the news caused consternation among US commanders. It was the first indication that the enemy was expanding into the southwest Pacific and now posed an immediate threat to Australia. On 7 August 1942, therefore, the US Marine Corps waded ashore on the fetid jungle-clad island to secure the incomplete airfield. In doing so they signalled the start of seven months of bitter fighting, much of it for possession of the airfield that the Americans called Henderson Field. The bloody campaign did not end until the last enemy soldier had finally been killed, the capture of Guadalcanal providing US forces with a much needed victory in the Pacific.

Among the units based on Guadalcanal were those equipped with the unconventional Lightning. Eight of the twin-engined, twin-boom fighters were flown in by pilots of the newly formed 339th FS/347th FG on 12 November. The next day another eight P-38Fs, assigned to the 39th FS/35th FG, flew in from Port Moresby, New Guinea, on loan from the Fifth Air Force – in mid-January 1943 the USAAF units on Henderson Field were subsumed into the Thirteenth Air Force.

In November the IJN suffered a series of defeats in the seas around the Solomons, easing the pressure on American troops on Guadalcanal. This meant that the eight 39th FS pilots could be sent back to New Guinea with seven of their P-38s on 22 November, the detachment having not actually seen any action. Further reinforcements would subsequently reach Henderson Field, with new Lightning pilots joining those already seasoned in operations.

Among those who would play a significant role while serving with the 339th FS during this time was 1Lt Douglas Canning. He made an interesting comment on the complexity of the fighter organisation on Guadalcanal during October-November 1942;

'On 15 September 15 pilots from the 70th FS [part of the 347th FG] in Fiji were transferred to the 67th FS [also assigned to the 347th FG], with future ace Capt John W Mitchell as the senior member. Most of us flew missions as 67th pilots and most were then assigned to the 339th when it was formed on 3 October. Also, the 67th's pilot strength had been augmented by those who'd been stationed in Hawaii, some joining the 67th and some the 339th. I was one of those who went to the 339th via the 67th from the 70th!'

P-38s of the 339th scored the type's first victories in the South Pacific whilst covering a strike on enemy shipping at Buin, on Bougainville island, on 18 November. Eleven B-17s and four B-24s were being escorted to the target by eight P-38s when 30 to 40 Japanese interceptors tried to break up the American attack. During the ensuing encounter no fewer than 17 Zero-sens were claimed as shot down, three of them by the 339th. Lt Delton Fincher claimed to have downed two and Lt James Obermiller one.

December brought a major change of fortune for the Americans when they were able to go on the offensive against the Japanese in the Solomons. The 70th FS's initial operations from Guadalcanal were also the first flown in the central Solomons by a unit from the 347th FG, which comprised the P-39- and P-38-equipped 67th, 68th, 70th and 339th FSs. The Lightnings were employed as fighter escorts for ground attack missions mounted by P-39s against the remaining Japanese forces on Guadalcanal.

Offensive operations over the northern Solomons continued on 10 December when 11 B-17s covered by eight P-38s attacked shipping in Buin-Faisi Harbour. The bombers claimed hits on a Japanese tanker while the P-38 pilots were credited with five Zero-sens destroyed. These included one each for Doug Canning and his wingman Delton Goerke.

1Lt Tom Lanphier also got his, and the 70th FS's, first confirmed Zero-sen kill on this date during a raid on Munda, which saw two Lightnings from the unit accompanied by a pair of P-38s from the 339th. Nine SBDs, nine P-39s, four P-38s and four F4F Wildcats had engaged 14 Zero-sens trying to intercept the American raiders, with the USAAF pilots reportedly downing five IJNAF fighters – Lanphier's was the only claim for the P-38s. Lanphier would of course subsequently play a key role in the Yamamoto mission of 18 April 1943.

On 14 December 1942 another of the pilots who would participate in the Yamamoto operation also claimed his first victory – while flying a P-39D. 1Lt Rex Barber of the 70th FS was always proud of the fact that he had shot down an enemy aircraft – a Mitsubishi G4M 'Betty' bomber – while flying the generally despised Bell fighter, and he would duplicate the feat in the coming months with a P-38 for much greater glory.

When the Thirteenth Air Force was formed in January 1943 it included two fighter groups, the 18th and 347th, with five P-39 squadrons as well as two P-40 squadrons and the P-38-equipped 339th FS. In addition, Detachment B of the 6th Night Fighter Squadron (NFS) would soon commence operations with Douglas P-70s and radar-equipped P-38s.

The Japanese were desperately trying to reinforce their own air forces in-theatre to the point that Mitsubishi F1M 'Pete' float-biplane reconnaissance aircraft were used for interception and A6M2-N 'Rufe' floatplane fighters were pressed into service as both bomber escorts and ground attack aircraft. A large number of Zero-sens were also rushed in from other theatres to fill the gap in Japanese defences in the Solomons, as well as to fly bomber escort missions.

With an increase in the number of enemy aeroplanes in the region, it was not long before Lightning pilots from the 339th began to claim aerial successes in January 1943. On the 5th, for example, the unit covered B-17s that were sent to attack a Japanese cruiser in the Bougainville area. They were met by a host of 'Petes' and 'Rufes', and one of the latter was downed by Capt John Mitchell for his first kill in a P-38 (he had claimed three victories in P-39s the previous autumn). Squadronmate and fellow future ace 1Lt Besby Holmes was credited with a 'Pete' destroyed for his first kill. Both would play an important role in the downing of Adm Yamamoto in the same area.

Mitchell, who had been the senior combat leader when the 339th was formed, engaged the enemy again on 27 January after nine Japanese Army

Air Force (JAAF) twin-engined Kawasaki Ki-48 'Lily' bombers, escorted by a number of Nakajima Ki-43 'Oscar' fighters, were intercepted over the Russell Islands. Six P-38s and eight F4Fs dived on the 'Oscars' from 20,000 ft, and in the ensuing melee, which also involved additional formations of P-40s and F4Fs, ten Ki-43s were reported to have been shot down. Mitchell claimed his fifth and sixth victories, making him the Thirteenth Air Force's first ace.

Two days later Mitchell received permission to try a night interception when a formation of 'Betty' bombers raided Guadalcanal after midnight. Observers on the ground were treated to the thrilling spectacle of the G4M's flaring exhausts merging with the bright tracers of Mitchell's guns before the intruder exploded in flames. It crashed to earth, signalling that he had gained his seventh victory. It would be the prelude to another interception that would be remembered for rather longer.

THE YAMAMOTO FACTOR

The Japanese abandoned Guadalcanal as quietly as they could in the middle of February 1943. So frustrating was the loss of this strategic outpost that desperate plans were considered in an attempt to regain the initiative. One, which had little chance of success in view of growing American strength in both the Solomon Islands and New Guinea, was known as Operation *I-Go*. It was an optimistic move that hurled bombing raids against Port Moresby, Oro Bay, Milne Bay and Guadalcanal during the second week of April.

After *I-Go* ended dismally for the Japanese, the commander-in-chief of the IJN, Adm Isoroku Yamamoto, decided to raise morale with a personal visit to forward bases. His schedule called for him to visit Bougainville on 18 April – a fact well known by US forces in the region after encrypted signals containing his itinerary had been intercepted and decoded. This information had been forwarded to Secretary of the Navy Frank Knox on the 16th. At first Knox disregarded the message, but when it was forwarded to President Franklin Roosevelt his response was immediate – 'Get Yamamoto'. Whether or not those were his actual words is open to debate,

Commander-in-chief of the IJN Adm Isoroku Yamamoto waves off Zero-sen fighters in this staged photograph, which was taken at Rabaul on 12 April 1943 – six days prior to his death in Operation *Vengeance*. A G4M1 'Betty' can be seen parked immediately behind Yamamoto (*Mikesh via Lansdale*)

but an order went out nevertheless to intercept and kill the man widely regarded as the architect of the Pearl Harbor attack and much of subsequent Japanese strategy.

On the 17th Knox sent an order to Adm Chester W Nimitz, the US Navy's Commander-in-Chief in the Pacific, that the aircraft carrying Yamamoto had to be intercepted and destroyed 'at all costs'. Knox's message added 'President attaches extreme importance to mission'. It was clear to senior military figures in Washington, D.C. that the only aircraft capable of making the interception were the 339th FS's Guadalcanal-based P-38s.

Accordingly, with all the speed that a modern industrial nation could muster, the Americans arranged for the USAAF and US Navy to cooperate on the planning and execution of a top-secret mission codenamed Operation *Vengeance*. Its aim was to intercept Yamamoto at Buin, the closest point in his itinerary to Henderson Field.

Special 310-gallon drop tanks were rushed out to Guadalcanal to enable the fighters to fly a 415-mile route to the interception point that would keep the P-38s out of sight of Japanese observers. It was, however, discovered that the Lightning could not accommodate two 300+ gallon external tanks. This meant that each fighter would carry one 310-gallon and one standard 165-gallon external tank – an arrangement that would provide sufficient fuel for the trip, with about 15 minutes of loiter time and enough for the return flight home.

Recently promoted Maj John Mitchell was the leader of the 16 P-38s that comprised the force for the flight to Bougainville. Capt Tom Lanphier and 1Lts Rex Barber, Besby Holmes and Raymond Hine made up the killer section that would attack the bombers carrying Yamamoto and his staff and deal with the escorting fighters. The remaining cover force included Maj Louis Kittel and 1Lts Doug Canning, Julius Jacobson, Delton Goerke, Gordon Whittaker, Roger Ames, Lawrence Graebner, Everett Anglin, William Smith, Eldon Stratton and Albert Long. At least six of these pilots already had victories to their credit, making the force a well-experienced one.

By 0725 hrs on the morning of 18 April 1943, 16 P-38s (two others were forced to abort at takeoff) had departed Henderson Field. The plan was for them to fly a circuitous route involving five separate legs to arrive over the target area at about 0935 hrs. When the P-38s reached Bougainville Doug Canning broke radio silence almost immediately to announce that he had sighted the objective. The following post-action report takes up the narrative, with the sections of the account that are either doubtful or inaccurate having been italicised;

'The Lightnings were at 30 ft, heading in toward the coast and just about to begin to get their altitude for the presumed attack. The enemy was sighted, in a "V", about three miles distant proceeding down the southern coast towards Kahili. The two bombers were together, flying at 4500 ft, with two sections of three Zeroes each 1500 ft above them and slightly to the rear.

'As the enemy force, apparently unaware of opposition, pursued its course, Mitchell led his covering group in their climb for altitude, ultimately reaching 15,000 to 18,000 ft, from which point they stood their protecting vigil. Lanphier led his force parallel to the enemy, flying in towards them at an indicated 200 mph in a 35-degree climb. The P-38s climbed at 2200 ft per minute. When level with the bombers and about two miles away, Lanphier and Barber dropped their belly tanks and swung in to the attack at 280 mph indicated. Holmes had difficulty in releasing his tank and Hine remained with him until he could do so.

'When Lanphier and Barber were within one mile of contact their attack was observed by the enemy. The bombers nosed down, *one starting a 360-degree turning dive* and the other going out and away toward the shoreline. The Zeroes dropped their belly tanks and three peeled down in a string to intercept Lanphier. When he saw that he could still reach the bomber he turned up and into the Zeroes, *exploding the first* and firing into the others as they passed. By this time he had reached 6000 ft, so he nosed over and went down to the treetops after his escaping objective. He came into it broadside and fired his bursts – *a wing flew off and the plane went flaming to earth.*

'The Zeroes were now pursuing him, and they had the benefit of altitude. His mission accomplished he hedgehopped the treetops and made desperate manoeuvres to escape. He kicked rudders and slipped and skidded, tracer flying past his plane, but he finally outran them. In all the action he had received two 7.7 mm bullets in his horizontal stabiliser.

'Barber had gone in with Lanphier on the initial attack. He went for one of the bombers but its manoeuvres caused him to overshoot a little. He whipped back, however, and although pursued by Zeroes, caught the bomber and destroyed it. When he fired, the tail section flew off and the bomber turned over onto its back and plummeted to earth.

'By this time Holmes had been able to drop his tank and with Hine, who had stayed in formation with him, came in to ward off the Zeroes who were pursuing Barber. A dogfight ensued and many shots were exchanged but results were not observed. The flight was on its way out of the combat area (in the neighbourhood of enemy bases at Kahili, Ballale and Shortland-Faisi) when Holmes noticed a stray bomber near Moila Point flying low over the water. *He dived on it, his bursts getting it smoking in the left engine – Hine also shot at it* and Barber polished it off with a burst to the fuselage. The bomber exploded "right in my [Barber's] face", a piece of the plane flew off, cut through his left wing and knocked out his left [inter]cooler. Other chunks left paint streaks on his wing – so close was his attack driven home.

'Holmes, Hine and Barber then turned for home, their mission – to destroy the bombers – having been a complete success. However, Zeroes were coming in on Barber's tail and Holmes whipped up and around *and shot one down in flames. Another attempt to draw away ended in another dogfight, during which Barber exploded a further Zero.* During these minutes, Hine's left engine started to smoke and he was last seen losing altitude south of Shortland Island. *It is believed that Hine also accounted for a Zero, as a total of three enemy fighters were seen to fall into the sea during this part of the combat.*

'Barber and Holmes were forced to use extreme evasive measures to escape from the enemy, and their course, as was Lanphier's, was further impeded by the sight of a huge cloud of dust fanning out from a swarm of planes taking off from Kahili airfield. Holmes eventually ran out of gas and made a successful emergency landing on the Russell Islands, from which he later brought his plane safely home to base. The damage to the cooling system of Barber's left engine prevented him from pulling more than 30 inches of mercury at low

1Lt Rex Barber flew 1Lt Bob Petit's P-38G-13 43-2204 on the famous Yamamoto mission, his regular Lightning having gone unserviceable 24 hours prior to the 18 April 1943 flight. Unofficially at least, the Barber/ *Miss Virginia* combination put up an extraordinary showing that day, downing both bombers and one of the Zero-sens that took off from Kahili. The official version, which gives him partial credit for both bombers, is still a remarkable record for even as skilled a pilot as Rex Barber

Officers involved with the Yamamoto mission gather for photographs several days later. They are, from left to right Lt Col H H Vicellio, Maj Tom Tyre, Capt Tom Lanphier, unknown, Gen Nathan Twining, Maj John Mitchell, Lt Rex Barber, Lt Jack Jacobson, Lt Besby Holmes, unknown, Lt Albert Long, Maj Lou Kittel, Lt Bill Smith, Lt Larry Graebner and Lt Roger Ames. The last five officers were members of 12th FS/18th FG, while the remaining pilots were from the 339th FS/347th FG (*Gen H H Vicellio files via Doug Canning*)

levels and 25 inches at 4000/5000 ft, but despite this limitation to his speed and rate of climb he also brought his plane safely home to base.'

Yamamoto's party had taken off from Rabaul in a G4M 'Betty' bomber of the 705th Kokutai at about the same time that John Mitchell was leading his P-38s westward from Guadalcanal. A second 'Betty' containing Adm Matome Ugaki and other members of Yamamoto's staff followed the first, and the two Japanese bombers flew together on the fatal route to Buin. Ironically, the defensive 7.7 mm and 20 mm ammunition carried by both aircraft had been reduced in order to save weight on the trip.

Overconfidence was perhaps also evident in the paucity of the escort detailed to cover the two bombers. Six A6M Zero-sens of the 204th Kokutai were led by Lt(jg) Takeshi Morisaki, and they flew in two groups of three, much to the surprise of the P-38 pilots in the attack section because such formations had long since been discarded by most air forces. The escort was taken completely by surprise when the Americans attacked from below the bombers. The Japanese pilots were searching ahead to the horizon and above in anticipation of the standard American tactic of striking from altitude. One of the Zero-sen pilots – Kenji Yanigawa – reported attacking a P-38 from the rear, breaking off only when he saw his opponent falling away with a smoking engine near Shortland Island. This fact suggested that it was possibly Yanigawa who shot down 1Lt Ray Hine. He was the only American pilot lost during the combat. Three other Zero-sen pilots claimed probables.

It is ironic that despite Operation *Vengeance* being both well planned and executed, it would ultimately have little effect on the Pacific war. Adm Mineichi Koga swiftly replaced Yamamoto as commander-in-chief of the Combined Fleet, and the Allies were obliged to adjust to an entirely new strategy and command technique. Perhaps the major accomplishment of the interception was to cover the American pilots in glory and to demonstrate the ability of the P-38 to do the job for which it was designed – long-range bomber interception.

Most of the Lightning pilots involved in Operation *Vengeance* had been in-theatre for some time, and it was considered prudent to remove them out of harm's way to avoid the risk of capture. Within weeks most were on the way home. Tom Lanphier had the most influence on the final mission debriefing, and he was not shy to embellish his part in the operation. This helped to make him the pilot most associated with its success. Of course, even the most cursory glance at the facts leads to the conclusion that John Mitchell and Rex Barber had each played vital roles in a remarkable operation.

After Yamamoto

In the second half of April and into May a pronounced lull fell over operations in the Solomon Islands as the Japanese were obliged to reorganise and evaluate their options following the failure of *I-Go*. Despite the tailing off of bomber raids, the IJNAF mounted a night attack on Henderson on 13 May when the crews of four 'Bettys' tried to penetrate the American defences. One bomber was caught in the searchlight beams and 1Lt William Smith took a P-38 up to score a victory for the 12th FS/8th FG. During this period the type was being worked up for operations with the 6th NFS, and an improvised radar-equipped Lightning was used to claim another nocturnal victory on 19 May.

Japanese efforts to reclaim the initiative in the South Pacific reached a climax of sorts on 16 June when 24 Aichi D3Y 'Val' dive-bombers from the 582nd Kokutai, escorted by 70 Zero-sens from the 582nd, 204th and 251st Kokutais, were sent down the Solomons 'slot' to attack shipping in the Guadalcanal area. The Allies responded with 104 interceptors, of which 76 engaged the Japanese raiders. A whopping 90+ claims were made by the American fighter pilots, which, if substantiated, would have more than wiped out the attacking force. Japanese records, however, document the loss of 13 'Vals' and 15 Zero-sens.

Between 1345 hrs and 1600 hrs the P-39s, Royal New Zealand Air Force-flown Kittyhawks, F4F Wildcats, F4U Corsairs and 12 P-38s from the 339th FS engaged the Japanese force as it pressed on towards Guadalcanal. 2Lt Bill Harris engaged a formation of Japanese fighters and fought them until his ammunition ran out. He reported shooting down two 'Zekes' before being forced to withdraw. Harris had also claimed two 'Zekes' nine days earlier, but he would have to wait until 4 October to 'make ace'.

The most remarkable performance of the day, however, was apparently that of 2Lt Murray Shubin, who already had a 'Rufe' and a 'Zeke' to his credit. He led his flight into the engagement over Beaufort Bay at 1345 hrs, and immediately claimed the destruction of two Zeroes, but he was alone when he sighted a formation of six more 'Zekes' below his altitude of 20,000 ft at around

The 339th FS's Lt Murray Shubin stands by his P-38G-13 43-2242 soon after completing his 'ace in a day' sortie on 16 June 1943. He had previously scored two kills prior to becoming the sole Lightning pilot in the Pacific to be officially credited with five victories in one combat. All of his victims on 16 June were 'Zekes'

Shubin poses with P-38H *Oriole Wuv*
(serial unknown), which he probably
used to claim his final four kills in
October 1943 (*Jack Cook*)

1400 hrs. Shubin made a daring run on the Japanese fighters – most likely from the 251st Kokutai, as that was the only Zero-sen unit to report engaging P-38s that day – and he claimed to have shot one of them down. Immediately climbing for altitude, he was surprised when he looked around to see the enemy fighters responding incoherently to his attack.

For the next 40 minutes Shubin engaged each of the Zero-sens individually, while the others made wild passes at him from behind. By the end of this wild battle he counted six enemy fighters as probably shot down, as they were trailing smoking black spirals across the sky. His altitude had now come down to 11,000 ft and, as most of his ammunition had been used, he prudently headed for home. Shubin's wingman, 2Lt Rake, had already retired from the battle by the time he engaged the six 'Zekes', Rake's aircraft having been damaged.

It is virtually impossible to disentangle the details of the battle on 16 June. As previously noted, the Japanese had 28 aircraft shot down, while six Allied fighters were lost in return. Shubin's victories were witnessed by Capt Mueller of the 35th Infantry, who watched the fight through field glasses from his vantage point on the ground in the Esperance-Savo area. No other record was available to corroborate Mueller's account, however, so the weight of his evidence is uncertain. The loss of seven Zero-sens, including one that ditched on the way home, was admitted by the 251st Kokutai. Pilots from the 339th claimed to have shot down 11 Japanese aircraft.

Murray Shubin's exploits during this mission gave him the distinction of being the only P-38 pilot in the Pacific to claim five Japanese aircraft in a single mission. Despite his derisive comment that the opposing pilots seemed especially 'inexperienced and stupid', the fact remained that he met a superior force of enemy fighters and defeated them decisively. Although several P-38 pilots would subsequently be able to claim four Japanese victories in a single engagement, none equalled Shubin's feat.

One conclusion that could be drawn from this engagement was that the Japanese dominance of the Southwest Pacific theatre was now on the decline, and the Allies would henceforth remain on the offensive for the rest of the war. Other islands in the Solomon chain would duly fall to American troops until the USAAF and US Navy were finally in a position to target the formidable Japanese bastion of Rabaul. Nevertheless, the Japanese did what they could to counter American pressure towards the north. To that end, IJN convoys continued to reinforce the defenders holding New Georgia. They were soon suffering heavy losses, however, with three destroyers being sunk on the night of 6 August 1943 alone. Other islands including Bougainville would fall to the Americans over the next few months.

With the skies during daylight hours bristling with Allied fighters, the IJNAF pinned its hopes on night bombing. To counter this growing threat, the 6th NFS deployed its improvised radar-equipped P-38s. The unit enjoyed a reasonable degree of success during this period, with 'Betty' bombers being intercepted over the Russell Islands and Guadalcanal itself on the night of 14/15 August. At about 2040 hrs on the 14th

1Lt James Harrell attacked a bomber at 21,000 ft from below over the Russells and shot it down in flames with a single burst. Squadronmate 2Lt Henry Meigs caught another 'Betty' over Guadalcanal that same night, the Japanese bomber being framed in the searchlight beams at about midnight. Meigs quickly shot it down to score the first of his six P-38 victories.

On 21 September Meigs would be up again to claim a pair of 'Bettys' in the night sky to the cheers of onlookers on the ground, who had a ringside seat as the contest was illuminated by searchlights. He would later transfer to the 339th FS and claim three Zero-sens in diurnal combat in early 1944. It is possible, however, that Meigs' three nocturnal victories make him the top-scoring P-38 nightfighter pilot.

The two future ranking Thirteenth Air Force P-38 aces enjoyed repeated aerial success in the final months of 1943. Bill Harris already had four claims to his credit when he escorted B-24s on a mission to Kahili on 4 October. Four Zero-sens were reportedly shot down over the target area, and one of these elevated Harris to ace status. Having claimed another 'Zeke' on 7 October, Harris really hit his stride on the 10th when he was credited with the destruction of three more Zero-sens (and a fourth as a probable) during two missions to Kahili and Choiseul.

On the Kahili trip Harris' wingman was the high-scoring Maj Bob Westbrook (CO of the 44th FS/18th FG), who was flying his first P-38 mission after claiming seven kills while flying P-40Fs between January and July 1943. He also destroyed a Zero-sen over Kahili. Finally, Murray Shubin was on the 10 October mission, and he claimed another two Zero-sens for his eighth and ninth victories.

The Japanese hold on Bougainville itself was threatened when the Stirling and Treasury Islands were invaded later in October. The IJNAF responded with attacks on US Navy transports anchored off the islands. One especially heavy assault was made on 27 October when new Yokosuka D4Y 'Judy' dive-bombers came down from the north. The 339th met one formation and claimed to have downed seven of them. Murray Shubin reported destroying two for his tenth and eleventh claims, while Bill Harris was credited with his tenth victory.

2Lt Henry Meigs, photographed with his P-38H-1 42-66686 some time between his service with the 12th and 339th FSs in late 1943, was one of the premier Lightning nightfighter pilots. He claimed three 'Betty' bombers in August and September 1943 while flying a modified P-38G of the 6th NFS in the early morning hours over Guadalcanal. Meigs subsequently 'made ace' in February 1944 while flying P-38Js with the 339th FS/347th FG over the Rabaul area in daylight hours (*Jack Cook*)

ATTACK ON RABAUL

With new airfields established on the recently won islands in the northern Solomon Islands, Allied aircraft were now able to reach the fortress of Rabaul. In fact, the Fifth Air Force had been attacking it from New Guinea throughout October and November 1943, and now the Thirteenth Air Force, US Navy, US Marine Corps, RNZAF and Royal Australian Air Force (RAAF) units were poised to continue the aerial offensive.

Bob Westbrook enjoyed a remarkable period of success over Rabaul in December flying with the 44th FS – the unit had been fully re-equipped with P-38s in November, although Westbrook had been flying Lightnings since 10 October. Having claimed a 'Zeke' on 23 December for his ninth victory, he enjoyed his best day in combat on Christmas Eve when the 44th escorted withdrawing B-24s past Cape St George, before turning back to hunt for pursuing Zero-sens. Westbrook's flight had sighted enemy fighters below them while orbiting above the bombers at 25,000 ft. In the ensuing melee P-38s and Zero-sens mingled like angry hornets. Westbrook fired and was fired on, but he managed to claim four 'Zekes' shot down (two were shared) without loss to his own formation. He was now both a P-40 and a P-38 ace, with his tally standing at 12 victories.

Christmas Day brought more success for Westbrook, as the following squadron report noted;

'Four flights of P-38s took off from Munda at 0945 hrs and proceeded northwest toward Rabaul. When over southeast New Ireland at 1200 hrs Maj Westbrook saw 18 "Zekes" almost over the town of Rabaul. Half of them peeled off to attack the bombers. The others broke up and started away from our planes. Maj Westbrook picked out the third Zero from the left and pursued it. It made a 180-degree turn and he sent several bursts towards it, seeing his tracers go into the fuselage. The "Zeke", as it completed the turn, went into a shallow dive. Maj Westbrook followed, firing until he was over on his back, at which point he saw flame and black smoke coming from the "Zeke's" engine cowling. Pulling up, with Flt Off Rex A Byers on his wing, he fired at several individual Zeros without observing results.

'Approaching Duke of York Island one Zero came around on Byers' tail. Maj Westbrook pulled up in the rear, fired and saw it go down in a slow spiral, then spin, smoking heavily and shedding pieces. At this point, Flt Off Byers shot one Zero off Maj Westbrook's tail and the latter saw both enemy planes make splashes in the sea to the east of Duke of York Island. At the completion of this action, Maj Westbrook's left engine started burning. He saw Flt Off Byers turn away from him and go into a cloud over Duke of

Maj Robert 'Westy' Westbrook, seen here later in the war, had been credited with 14 confirmed victories by the end of 1943 – seven of them achieved while flying P-38s with the 44th FS/18th FG (*USAF*)

York Island, pursued by three Zeros, his right engine smoking and leaking Prestone. This was the last time Flt Off Byers was seen. In striving to reach the clouds Maj Westbrook, now attacked by several "Zekes", was joined by an F4U (flown by Lt Firestone), which dispersed the enemy planes. Maj Westbrook cut all switches, the fire in the right engine was somehow extinguished and he returned to Barakoma, landing at 1430 hrs.'

Westbrook subsequently became deputy CO of the 347th FG in May 1944, and he had increased his tally to 20 victories by the time he was killed while on a strafing mission in November 1944.

Rabaul was effectively abandoned by the Japanese in March 1944. By then the Thirteenth Air Force was virtually entirely P-38-equipped as part of XIII Fighter Command, and in June 1944 it was combined with the Fifth Air Force to form the Far East Air Forces (FEAF) under the command of Maj Gen George Kenney. The FEAF, whose fighter groups in the main flew Lightnings through to war's end, would play a key role in the liberation of the Philippines and the subsequent campaign in Southeast Asia.

NEW GUINEA – THE FIGHTER PILOTS' WAR

Maj Gen George Kenney was commanding the California-based Fourth Air Force when he was chosen to head the newly formed Fifth Air Force in New Guinea. He arrived in July 1942 and proceeded, like a whirlwind, to create an effective air force out of the wreckage of the defeated and disorganised components then existing in the Southwest Pacific. Confident and energetic, Kenney would be considered a smart operator by those he would lead into combat.

One of his innovations was large-scale use of the P-38. He had already gained first-hand experience of the Lockheed fighter while heading up the Fourth Air Force, which was not only the primary air defence command for the West Coast but it also controlled the major training units for the type. Accordingly, Kenney made sure that the Lightning would be expeditiously introduced into Fifth Air Force service by V Fighter Command units, which were manned by the best pilots available. One such individual that he took care to assign to his new command was a quiet, tow-headed youngster from Wisconsin who would become America's ranking fighter ace of all time. His name was Richard Ira Bong.

Kenney and Bong initially met under less than happy circumstances shortly before the former left for the Pacific in July 1942. Bong and another New Guinea-bound pilot (and future ace), John 'Jump' O'Neill, had been hauled up before the Fourth Air Force commander for their boyish pranks on training flights. The exuberant O'Neill had flown loops around the Golden Gate Bridge, while Bong was reported to have flown so low over Market Street that secretaries working in offices there could clearly see him waving at them from his cockpit. He had also flown low enough to sweep clothes from a washing line. Kenney read Bong the riot act and ordered him to report to the offended housewife to help her re-hang the washing. As a veteran fighter pilot, however, Kenney also recognised the spirit and skill of the two young men, and made a mental note to ensure they were on the list of pilots destined for his new P-38 units.

Kenney was hopeful that the P-38 would be the key to his strategy of taking the measure of Japanese fighter potential. He knew that the enemy's bomber threat depended on fighter protection to make it effective. If the 150 to 200 Japanese fighters in the area could be neutralised, Kenney reasoned, the bombers would lack effective protection. He knew that the P-38 was the best Allied fighter in-theatre at that time, and he was eager to get as many of them into action as possible in order to secure air superiority. At first, though, there were frustrating delays caused by

Capt Curran 'Jack' Jones poses with his P-38F at Port Moresby in early 1943. He finished his tour in April 1943 and returned home two months later ('Jack' Jones)

mechanical problems like leaking cooling systems and defective superchargers. These technical maladies were compounded by a lack of maintenance experience in the frontline.

The first V Fighter Command units to receive the P-38 earned that honour on perhaps nothing more than the flip of a coin. It really was a fortunate choice, no matter the means of making it. The 39th FS had been praised for the way it had battled elite Japanese fighter units during the struggle to halt the enemy advance on Port Moresby in June-July 1942. The unit's pilots claimed to have shot down ten Japanese aircraft for the loss of an identical number of P-39 Airacobras. And although no 39th pilots were listed as killed, several were wounded or had fallen ill to malaria or typhus.

One of the wounded aviators was future 20-kill ace 1Lt Thomas Lynch, who was recovering from scrub typhus as well as a broken arm – an injury he had suffered when he had had to ditch his battle-damaged P-39 on 16 June 1942. Lynch, who had been credited with three victories while flying the Airacobra, would go on to become a P-38 ace and one of the great combat leaders of the war prior to his death in combat on 8 March 1944.

Lack of experience with the new P-38 initially plagued the 39th's pilots. Squadron veteran, and future ace, 1Lt 'Jack' Jones reported that when he

23

took a Lightning up for a high-altitude familiarisation test his pitot tube froze up, making it impossible for him to know his airspeed. Worried that it would prevent a safe landing, Jones searched for the pitot-heating switch without success. Flying at a lower and warmer altitude unfroze the pitot head, allowing him to land – and continue his search for the relevant control. After 30 minutes sitting in his cockpit on the ground Jones finally located the switch, which was hidden from view behind the control wheel.

2Lt Richard Bong had been assigned to the 9th FS/49th FG in October 1942, and upon his arrival in-theatre he went on loan to the 39th FS/35th FG to help impart his Lightning experience to the recently re-equipped unit. Having provided its pilots with whatever knowledge he could Bong stayed on, and in doing so helped write some impressive operational history with the neophyte P-38 unit. 2Lt Stanley Andrews was another young Lightning pilot fresh from the US who provided the 39th FS with some clues on operating the type. He remembered helping groundcrews refit ailerons that had been installed on the wrong wings of a newly assembled P-38 in Port Moresby, New Guinea.

INITIAL P-38 VICTORY

Somehow, under the leadership of Maj Gen Kenney and his staff, the P-38 became operational from New Guinea in October 1942. Patrols and reconnaissance missions were the main sorties initially scheduled. Alerts in reaction to the nightly routine of Japanese bombing and a few escort missions for Allied bombers failed to satisfy the 39th's eagerness for combat, however. One promising diversion presented itself when eight squadron pilots (Lts Faurot, King, Sparks, Rohrer, Lane, Denton, Schifflett and Flagler) were sent on detached service to Guadalcanal on 14 November. They duly spent a tense few days on the besieged island until the immediate threat posed by enemy forces passed, the pilots then flying their Lightnings back to Port Moresby on the 22nd without them having actually encountered the enemy.

This P-38F (serial unknown) was possibly the fighter flown by Capt Bob Faurot of the 39th FS/35th FG when he was posted on detached duty from Port Moresby to Guadalcanal in November 1942. Indeed, he probably used it to make his remarkable claim of downing a Zero-sen with a bomb that same month

Capt Bob Faurot of the 39th FS/35th FG poses with his distinctively marked P-38F at Port Moresby in early 1943. He was lost in the same action that saw pioneer P-38 ace 1Lt Hoyt Eason killed on 3 March 1943

But Bob Faurot did find action a few days later. One of the routine operations provided an opportunity for combat with the Japanese on 25 November when six of the squadron's pilots were scheduled to dive-bomb Lae with 500-lb weapons. They found the enemy ready for them when they reached the target area. On previous missions to Lae the 39th FS pilots had reportedly taunted the Japanese, challenging them to 'come up and fight us if you dare'. The squadron diary kept by SSgt Donald Thomas describes what happened during the action on the 25th;

'Faurot, Lynch, Jones, Shifflett, Lane and Sparks took off loaded with 500-lb bombs for a dive-bombing mission to Lae at 0950 hrs. Shifflet had supercharger trouble 20 miles short of Lae and returned, but the others arrived and began their runs from west to east along the runway, starting the attacks at 17,000 ft and pulling out at 4000 ft. As Faurot began his run he observed a "Zeke" taking off from the strip, and turned to intercept the enemy plane. Remembering he still had his bombs, he dropped them and the "Zeke" passed over the ordnance just as it exploded in the water, flipping the Jap fighter over and causing it to crash into the sea.

'Tom Lynch dropped both of his bombs in the hangar area at the seaward end of the runway, destroying a building. Lane hit the same area with his bombs. Jones' bombs struck the dispersal area at the northwestern end of the runway. Faurot made another strafing run and, as he turned back, ran into two "Zekes" at about 3000 ft. He fired a quick burst at the first plane but missed. He turned head-on into the No 2 "Zeke" and began firing, observing hits as the Jap flew into his fire. All our aircraft arrived home safely at 1145 hrs. Not a bad day!'

A total of nine Zero-sens had managed to get airborne at Lae at around 1030 hrs when the P-38s attacked, including six from the 582nd Kokutai and three others from the 252nd. Japanese records indicate that the aircraft encountered four P-38s, but there were no results and no claims made. Other members of the flight witnessed Faurot's bizarre method of destroying an enemy aircraft and reported what they saw. Jack Jones saw the Zero-sen do a 180-degree turn and splash into the sea off the end of the runway to provide some solid evidence for the claim. Kenney personally chided Faurot, telling him he wanted enemy aircraft shot down not doused with water. Nevertheless, he awarded Faurot with a medal for his efforts.

The end of November and beginning of December represented a period of inactivity while the 39th stood down for the overhaul of its aircraft. When operations resumed during the second week of December it seemed to herald another round of fruitless patrols and scrambles against 'ghost' Japanese bombing raids. The monotony was broken with a scramble on 27 December after a period of bad weather that had restricted flying. About 30 to 40 Zero-sens, 'Oscars' and 'Val' dive-bombers were reported over Buna, about 20 minutes flying time to the north of Port Moresby. Tom Lynch led Red Flight aloft from 14-Mile Drome at 1130 hrs, his formation consisting of Lightnings flown by John Mangas, Dick Bong and Ken Sparks. Behind Red Flight a further eight P-38s would fall in behind Tom Lynch, although his original flight of four fighters were the first to engage the Japanese force.

Fighter control reported the presence of only two Zero-sens, but Red Flight ran into 12 of the fighters. They were also accompanied by 12 'Vals' of the 582nd Kokutai and no fewer than 31 'Oscars' of the 11th Sentai. The Japanese force had been sent south from Rabaul to strafe and bomb the new American airfield at Dobodura.

Some of the Japanese fighters had begun their strafing attacks when a flight of 9th FS P-40s sighted part of the enemy formation at 14,000 ft. The P-40 leader radioed Lynch that there were 'Zekes' dead ahead, and the P-38 pilot observed a formation of about 20 to 30 fighters, which he quickly identified as 'Oscars'. It was an astute judgment considering that the Nakajima fighter had been operating in the New Guinea area for only about a week. Lynch could see that the 'Oscars' had dark brown camouflage with large red Hinomaru insignia on the wings and fuselages, and that they were in four-ship elements, all flying in trail. He promised to drive the Japanese fighters down to the 9th FS formation at 7000 ft.

Lynch clearly had the initiative over the enemy machines, with an altitude advantage of at least 5000 ft and the element of surprise. Red Flight bounced one four-ship 'Oscar' group without result. Lynch then pulled up to the left, whereupon he sighted a P-38 with three 'Oscars' on its tail. This Lightning was probably aircraft 41-2631, flown by future ace 2Lt Ken Sparks. Lynch fired at an enemy fighter, which fell away towards the sea trailing smoke. This was probably the aircraft of Sgt Kurihara, who later reported to have suffered a damaged engine and fuel tank. Although the aircraft was proving difficult to control, Kurihara managed to coax it back to New Britain, where the engine quit. He crash-landed on a small peninsula at Talasea. An IJNAF flying boat brought Kurihara back to Rabaul the following evening.

1Lt Ken Sparks of the 39th FS/ 35th FG claimed 11 victories between 27 December 1942 and 21 July 1943, when he finished his tour. He was killed in a flying accident on 5 September 1944 whilst serving as a P-38 flying instructor in California

1Lt Hoyt Eason of 39th FS/35th FG was the first P-38 ace to emerge in the Southwest Pacific, claiming two 'Zekes' on 27 December and three more four days later. Credited with a sixth kill on 8 January 1943, Eason was posted missing in action over the Bismarck Sea on 3 March 1943

Meanwhile, Sparks tangled with several 'Oscars' before receiving hits in his left engine. Escaping in a steep dive, he decided to leave the battle. He was attempting to land his damaged fighter when a 'Val' crossed his sights. Sparks fired the rest of his ammunition at it and ground observers watched the dive-bomber fall, smoking, into the sea. Lynch claimed two 'Oscars' destroyed, one of which was seen to crash into the water. The latter aircraft was possibly flown by WO Yoshitake, who was the only JAAF pilot reported missing from the 11th Sentai formation. After landing at Port Moresby Lynch urged the startled groundcrews to prepare another P-38 because, as he put it, 'the sky is full of Japs over Buna!'

John Mangas was flying Charles King's aircraft when he attacked a Japanese fighter prior to being forced to avoid others coming up behind him. He was excited enough to mistake two P-40s for Japanese fighters, but fortunately for them his attack did no damage. Mangas left Buna after fighter control ordered all fighters home at 1300 hrs.

Dick Bong had dropped his external tanks and brashly made a single-handed attack on a Japanese fighter without result before he too was forced to evade others coming in behind him. He fired futilely at a 'Val', but the next one he targeted burst into flames from one of his bursts fired at 350 yards and then it fell into the sea. A Zero-sen then passed ahead of Bong at close range and he fired a short burst into it, which other squadron witnesses claimed sent the Japanese fighter down.

Yellow Flight had engaged the enemy aircraft from the east, being led into combat by future ace 1Lt Charles Gallup. He was saved from an attack by Japanese fighters when Carl Planck fired at one of them, the enemy machine exploding after a few bursts. Gallup then saw another Japanese fighter overshoot him, which he fired at until it was observed to crash in flames.

1Lt Hoyt Eason was leading White Flight, and he followed Lynch into the battle. He quickly caught one Japanese fighter and watched his fire hit its cockpit before the aircraft fell into the ocean. Eason then went to the rescue of a P-40 that was being attacked by another Japanese fighter. The Warhawk pilot later gratefully confirmed the destruction of his opponent when Eason shot it off his tail. Stanley Andrews, who was flying 'Trapeze White Three', observed the tail of the Zero-sen he was attacking disintegrate and fall off before the fighter itself spiralled down into the sea. Both Eason and Andrews would become aces.

From the American point of view the aerial engagement on 27 December had been a great victory for the P-38. Eleven Japanese aircraft were confirmed as shot down, with three others heavily damaged and probably shot down. Kenney was so anxious to encourage initiative and aggressiveness that he upped the total claims confirmed to 15! The Japanese, however, acknowledged the loss of only two 'Oscars' and a single 'Val', and that another example of each type had crash-landed back at Rabaul. As nothing is known about the condition of these aircraft, the final total of Japanese casualties can be no more than five aircraft and possibly three aircrew. Sparks' fighter was the only P-38 to be seriously damaged, and it was subsequently repaired and returned to service.

On 31 December the 39th escorted A-20s, B-25s and B-26s to Lae for another strike on the Japanese base. The P-38s were at 15,000 ft, nearing the target when 12 Japanese fighters were sighted far below them. In the

action that followed Tom Lynch claimed two Zero-sens for his third and fourth P-38 victories. 2Lt John 'Shady' Lane watched Lynch's first victim explode, then claimed a fighter for himself in a head-on attack.

During this same engagement Hoyt Eason reported destroying three Zero-sens around Lae airstrip to become the first P-38 ace in the Southwest Pacific. Ken Sparks attacked another fighter that was making a slow roll, watching it crash into the jungle a few miles northeast of Lae. He then faced another determined Japanese pilot in a head-on attack until the two aircraft collided. Sparks' P-38 suffered a crushed wingtip, whilst the Japanese fighter was observed to go in with part of its wing missing. The enemy aircraft was probably an 'Oscar' of the 11th Sentai flown by Capt Hironojo Shishimoto, who reported bailing out of his fighter after ramming a P-38 in this area on this date. He returned to combat after claiming that his opponent had become one of his seven confirmed victories.

Following this action over Lae the 39th was credited with another nine kills to take its tally past 20 with the P-38. Irrespective of the *actual* total of victories, morale was extremely high in the squadron. The Lightning was on the threshold of its greatest period of fame.

LAE RE-SUPPLY CONVOYS

By January the besieged Japanese garrison at Lae was desperate for supplies and reinforcements. In order to rectify this situation, between 5 and 10 January 1943 five merchant ships sailed from New Britain to Lae, with aerial support provided by 'Oscars' of the 11th Sentai. Four vessels got through, but 23 Japanese fighters and six pilots, including 1Lt Hiroatsu Hirano and 2Lt Kotobuki Nagayo, were lost.

On 6 January the 39th returned to Lae to make a disappointing dive-bombing attack on the convoy. Stanley Andrews confessed his lack of ability at this form of attack. 'I was pretty lousy at dive-bombing. About all I ever did was get near misses that helped wash the ships down'. Other squadron members were equally inexperienced, so the fighter pilots had little to show for their efforts. But once they had dropped their bombs it was a different story. When they engaged the 11th Sentai they claimed nine 'Oscars' for no loss. Old hand Curran Jones added two, while Richard Smith,

P-38F-5 42-12652 exhibits signs of combat damage (right wingtip and trailing edge) after it was damaged in a collision with a Zero-sen on 31 December 1942 – the latter crashed near Lae airfield, being credited as the second of two kills to future 11-victory ace 2Lt Ken Sparks of the 39th FS/35th FG. An extremely aggressive pilot who claimed four victories in his first two engagements (on 27 and 31 December 1942), Sparks paid a price for his determination as his aircraft was the only one to receive serious damage on both occasions (*Krane Files*)

Capt Charlie 'Meatball' Sullivan (O'Sullivan from 1973) initially flew P-39 and P-400s with the 39th FS/ 35th FG, and claimed a bomber in one in June 1942. He then switched to the P-38 and gained four victories, two probables and a damaged with the fighter between 6 January and 26 July 1943. He later endured a 23-day trek back to safety after crash-landing his battle-damaged P-38 in Markham Valley during a mission to Wewak in September 1943

This well-weathered P-38F-5 (almost certainly 42-12621) of the 39th FS/ 35th FG was routinely flown by Capt Curran 'Jack' Jones. Seen here in the early spring of 1943, the fighter was used by Jones to claim all four of his Lightning kills between 2 January and 3 March. These gave him ace status when combined with a Zero-sen that he had downed on 9 June 1942 while flying a P-400 ('Jack' Jones)

Charles Sullivan, Richard Suehr and Stanley Andrews each claimed one. All five pilots would duly attain ace status.

The next day saw further engagements over the convoy, this time involving Zero-sens of the 252nd and 282nd Kokutais as well as the 'Oscars' of the 11th Sentai. The 39th's pilots claimed seven more enemy aircraft shot down. This time four Zero-sens were actually lost, although it is not clear to which American units. Ken Sparks claimed one 'Oscar' to record his fifth victory, while Dick Bong claimed two others to reach four. Charles Gallup downed two 'Oscars' and 'Shady' Lane accounted for another. Tom Lynch was credited with the final victory, the 'Oscar' he destroyed being his fifth success in the P-38 and his eighth overall. He also claimed an enemy transport vessel sunk when he strafed one of the ships. A B-17 crew saw the vessel burst into flames and then explode when the bomber went in to finish it off.

Japanese records claim the loss of a number of American raiders, but all the P-38s from the 39th FS returned to base. So far the squadron had been credited with the destruction of more than 30 Japanese aircraft without the loss of a single Lockheed fighter in combat.

Whatever successes the Allied air forces may have achieved in the air, the majority of the Japanese ships reached Lae late on 7 January to deliver approximately 4000 troops. The 39th FS was up again just after 0700 hrs the next day when 15 P-38s escorted RAAF Beaufighters and B-25s sent out to target the convoy. Several near misses and one direct hit were observed before the attackers withdrew. 'Oscars' tried to intercept the bombers but the P-38s dived on them from 17,000 ft, meeting the enemy fighters at 8000 ft. Four 'Oscars' were claimed destroyed, a fifth one was probably destroyed and a sixth damaged. Bob Faurot was credited with shooting down his second Japanese fighter, while Sparks got another, as well as claiming the probable. 'Shady' Lane also claimed a kill and Andrew Kish accounted for the fourth. Sparks' combat report is indicative of his enthusiasm during the fight;

'On our first pass I knocked one Zero off of Lt Kish's tail. He went down and out. I saw about a yard of orange-red flame shoot out from behind his cockpit. I saw my flight leader, Capt Faurot, shoot down one enemy plane on that first pass. In addition to this I saw three Zeroes – my

own, Capt Faurot's and another – hit the water when I pulled up to gain altitude. Later, I saw one hit the water west of the convoy. I fired on my probable toward the end of the fight.'

A second mission left at 1320 hrs when 12 P-38s escorted B-25s, B-26s, A-20s and Beaufighters in another attack on the transports. Several hits and near misses were again observed, and the A-20s and Beaufighters then strafed the aerodrome at Lae. Spotting 'Oscars' below them, the P-38s dived from 14,000 ft to attack – the American pilots subsequently claimed to have shot down five, with three others probably destroyed.

The day's third mission proved even more fruitful for the 39th FS, eight P-38s having sortied at 1705 hrs to escort B-17s headed for Lae. Richard Suehr got two 'Zekes' to take his tally to four victories, one of them having attacked him head-on. Suehr saw the enemy fighter explode in flames and head down towards the sea, only for Dick Bong to dive after it and claim the seemingly doomed aircraft as his fifth victory! Interestingly, Bong, in his combat report,

Capts Tom McGuire and Dick Bong were the ranking P-38 aces in the Pacific by the end of 1943, and although neither pilot would survive the war, they were still at the very top of the list come VJ Day. Bong's score stood at 21 kills on 31 December 1943, whilst McGuire had 16 victories to his name

claimed that his opponent was flying an 'Oscar'. His terse account reveals the way his mind was working during this significant moment in his combat career;

'Diving from the front, head-on, with about 30 degrees deflection. Two passes the same way. Second time he started spinning down out of control in Huon Gulf about five miles off the coast. Saw another "Oscar" spinning down through the hole in the clouds into Huon Gulf. Lt Walters shot it down at about 11,000 ft. Zeroes were waiting for the bombers to get to Lae, and they attacked before we reached them. Their warning system is either better or they are maintaining patrols.'

Bong had been flying Capt Charles King's P-38F-5 42-12653 on this occasion, rather than 42-12624 that he had used the previous day. Tom Lynch and King had been working on minor improvements to 42-12653 in order to increase the fighter's performance. Lynch was a proficient engineer, and his enhancements included relocating the gun camera from the P-38's nose to the left wing shackle. Accordingly, King's fighter was highly sought after by 39th pilots, and several, including Bong and Hoyt Eason, scored victories while flying it.

It was during this third mission of the day that Ken Sparks made his seventh victory claim. He had been one of the most exuberant of the squadron's pilots, and many of his kills came after he had ignored unit policy. This trait often saw Sparks at odds with his superiors, but like many high-scoring pilots before him, he claimed victories by flouting the rules.

Some valuable lessons were learned during this operation against escorted enemy shipping convoys. For one thing, it was clear that bomber attacks from altitude were generally ineffective against manoeuvring vessels. Maj Gen Kenney also decided that P-38s were better employed as interceptors rather than as dive-bombers since very little damage was done

39th FS/35th FG P-38F-5 42-12653 received special attention by the engineering-oriented aces Charlie King and Tom Lynch during 1943 at Port Moresby. The latter introduced technical innovations that made the fighter slightly faster and more responsive, giving it an edge in aerial combat. Although 42-12653 was assigned to Capt Charlie King, who claimed one of his five victories with it, the Lightning was also used by fellow aces Dick Bong and Hoyt Eason to claim early successes in 1942-43 (Charles King)

by their bombs. On the other hand, the bomber crews were grateful for the relief resulting from the fighters' intervention. The P-38 was proving most efficient in providing high altitude protection. Nevertheless, the Fifth Air Force began developing a new tactic for use by Lightnings performing the ground attack role.

Skip-bombing, or dropping bombs at wave-top height enabled them to skip on the surface of the sea and slam into the side of a ship. Mounting additional 0.50-in machine guns in the noses and onto the fuselage sides of A-20s and B-25s created improvised gunships that overwhelmed ships' anti-aircraft defences long enough for bombs to be dropped.

The P-38 had clearly proven its value as a fighter during operations over Lae, the aircraft's performance at higher altitudes giving the Lightning a huge advantage over its Japanese opponents. The neophyte 39th FS pilots had gained valuable combat experience, and they had also heeded sound advice given to them from veterans like Tom Lynch and Charles King. This information had allowed the unit to maximise the effectiveness of the P-38. Newcomers to the type began to realise that the Lightning could both out-climb and out-dive the Zero-sen, and that the Lockheed fighter could fly at higher altitudes to guarantee an initial tactical advantage. Additionally, it was clear that the P-38 possessed devastating firepower, which could tear the lightly constructed Japanese fighters apart with a single burst. And the twin-boom interceptor was sturdily built in the tradition of American combat aircraft, which meant that it was able to withstand the initial effects of Japanese firepower. These would be devastating factors in resisting the next Japanese attempt to reinforce Lae.

In the meantime other units would convert to the P-38 using stocks that Maj Gen Kenney had carefully husbanded. The first Fifth Air Force Lightning combat loss had occurred on the third mission of the 8 January operations. Several P-38s had also been damaged, but they were repaired to enable them to remain operational and give Kenney the opportunity to reform the 49th FG's 9th FS (then flying P-40Es) in January and the 8th FG's 80th FS (equipped with P-39s and P-400s) by March 1943.

The current priority on North Africa meant that all available P-38s were assigned to the Twelfth Air Force, but the ever-enterprising Maj Gen Kenney insisted that his fighter command be equipped with as many of the type as he could possibly muster.

Throughout the rest of January and into February the Japanese frantically assembled another convoy for the relief of Lae. Eager to avoid a repeat of the costly events of January, the enemy was content to use approaching bad weather as cover for the movement of ships across the Bismarck Sea to Vitiaz Strait – the stretch of water between New Britain and the Huon Peninsula. In late February the eight transports and their eight escorting destroyers slipped under the umbrella of cloud and rain and headed for Lae. This furtive action proved to be futile, however, because the convoy was sighted by an Allied aerial reconnaissance aircraft on 1 March. From then the Japanese ships were shadowed until the first hastily-assembled bombing force was able to sink one of the transports the following day at the start of an action that became known as the Battle of the Bismarck Sea.

Fifteen of the 39th's P-38s battled through the miserable weather as escorts for the bombers, the Lightning pilots sighting three 'Oscars' above the murk. One of the Japanese fighters quickly dived into the heavy cloud cover, but 2Lt Wilmot Marlett despatched a second machine and Capt Charles King downed the third, its pilot for some reason having decided to pull up into a virtual stall. Japanese sources acknowledge the loss of two fighters in this location at this time. For once the claims matched the actual losses.

More persistent attacks were made on the convoy on 3 March. During the initial main assault a force of 32 B-25s, 17 B-17s, 12 A-20s and 13 RAAF Beaufighters, escorted by 28 P-38s of the 9th and 39th FSs, attacked the vessels off Cape Ward Hunt in bad weather at 1015 hrs. Three transports were sunk and the remaining four were left burning. One of the escorting destroyers was also sunk. Zero-sens of the 204th Kokutai reported engaging P-38s that were barring their way to the bombers. Two IJNAF pilots, PO2c Shizuki Nishiyama and Chief Flyer Gansuke Yagashira, were listed as missing after the battle. Seven P-38s and a P-39 were claimed to have been shot down, although the P-39 may have been mistaken for a P-40 that was damaged during the battle.

Only the pilots of the 253rd Kokutai managed to engage the skip-bombers at low altitude, and they may have lost as many as three Zero-sens while claiming three A-20s and three P-38s destroyed. Other Zero-sen pilots from the aircraft carrier *Zuiho* reported shooting down two B-17s and a P-38 while losing two of their own.

Dick Bong, who had returned to the 9th from the 39th on 11 January, played a part in this mission, having been assigned to suppress enemy fighters that scrambled from airfields surrounding Lae. He scored his sixth victory when he claimed to have shot down an 'Oscar', with another, last seen descending with fuel leaking from its tanks, as a probable. At about the same time future ten-kill ace 1Lt Paul Stanch of the 39th scored his first victories while he tried to cover the P-38 flown by his CO, Maj George Prentice – they were probably engaged by Zero-sens of the 204th Sentai. Prentice apparently became overly aggressive while going after an IJNAF fighter, charging straight at the enemy aircraft. Stanch later reported;

1Lt Richard 'Snuffy' Smith scored seven victories while serving with the 39th FS/35th FG between 6 January and 22 September 1943. He claimed the last of these kills in this aircraft, P-38H-1 42-66532. Note that the name displayed on the nose (*Japanese Sandman II*) of Smith's fighter is festooned with Japanese flags

'We met 30 Zeroes at 18,000 ft, and because my motors were acting up and I knew I could climb no higher, I attacked. I saw Prentice fighting a Zero while another crept around behind him. I attacked this one, and got in a fine short burst when he turned in front of me. I followed him down to 8000 ft and watched him splash into the sea. I saw three of our bombers attacking and four other fighters beyond them, which turned out to be more Zeroes. A Zero shadowing our bombers failed to see me on his tail. I gave him a two-second burst and he erupted in flames.'

Stanley Andrews, Tom Lynch and Richard 'Snuffy' Smith each got one enemy fighter apiece, the 39th claiming ten Japanese aircraft destroyed to make it one of the unit's most successful days in combat in terms of aerial victories. However, the squadron had paid a heavy price for these kills, as Capt Bob Faurot and 1Lts Fred Schifflett and Hoyt Eason had all perished – the latter was the first P-38 ace to be killed in-theatre. The hard-fighting Faurot had led his flight to the defence of a B-17 under attack, but all three fighters plus the bomber had been lost.

Another attack on the remnants of the convoy was undertaken during the afternoon of 3 March. Both the surviving vessels and their fighter escorts suffered heavy casualties. By the end of the day all the transports and their destroyer escorts had either been sunk or heavily damaged. Japanese sources state that ten Zero-sens and an unknown number of 'Oscars' were lost. American sources claim that at least 25 Japanese fighters were shot down by the P-38 and P-40 squadrons involved. Even though it may be prudent to discount 20 to 40 per cent of American claims, it is clear that the effectiveness of Japanese air power in-theatre was now on the decline.

The grisly business of mopping up the convoy continued on 4 and 5 March, with the sinking of any remaining ships and the strafing of survivors in the water. Some of the Japanese troops were rescued by their comrades and transported back to Rabaul, but only around 1200 of the 6900 soldiers that had been embarked in the transports arrived in the Lae area. The decision to reinforce the New Guinea front had clearly been a mistake. This convoy battle had proven just how effective the P-38 was as a fighter.

P-38Fs from the 39th FS/35th FG are seen lined up in the open at Port Moresby in early February 1943. 1Lt Charles Gallup's 42-12627 is parked closest to the camera at right. The unit had swapped its Airacobras for Lightnings in November 1942, and by the beginning of 1943 its official score stood at 20 aerial victories. Thanks to an escalation in aerial combat, the 39th FS had generated five P-38 aces by the second week of January (*National Archives*)

– OPERATION *I-GO* – BEYOND DESPERATION –

Pressure on Lae became intense after the Allied victory during the Battle of the Bismarck Sea. The 39th FS's diary records several days of escorting transports to the forward base at Wau, before again covering bombing missions to Lae from 16 March. Attacks on the bases around Wewak also commenced on the 18th, thus placing the entire northeastern coast of New Guinea beyond the Huon peninsula under the threat of aerial assault.

Adm Yamamoto had been painfully aware that the Japanese perimeter south of Rabaul was now under pressure, and he was urged to react by senior officers in Japan who felt that it was imperative to at least parry the Allied advance. For Yamamoto part of the answer was to regain the initiative by bombing Guadalcanal and Port Moresby, as well as other forward Allied bases in eastern New Guinea and the northern Solomon Islands. The Japanese counterattack, codenamed Operation *I-Go*, began on 7 April with raids on Guadalcanal.

New Guinea got its first taste of the new offensive on the 11th when a formation of 45 Japanese aircraft was intercepted by all three squadrons now equipped with the P-38, plus P-40s of the 49th FG. By the end of this one-sided clash the USAAF pilots claimed 17 Japanese aircraft destroyed for the loss of a single P-40. On the ground, an Allied freighter and the new wharf at Oro Bay had been hit.

The 80th FS had its first contact with the enemy as a P-38 unit during the 11 April engagement. Combat veteran Capt Danny Roberts was leading the four aircraft of the squadron's 'Ping Pong Red' Flight, he and his pilots emerging from the fight with claims for a Zero-sen and three 'Val' dive-bombers destroyed without loss. Roberts' combat report contained some illuminating descriptions of the battle;

'I took off at 1210 hrs with "Ping Pong Red", climbed at full power after checking our radios and headed for Porlock Harbor as ordered. Reached 20,000 ft just south of Oro Bay at 1235 hrs and flew up-sun and very close to cloud formation, reaching 25,000 ft. Eighteen to 20 dive-bombers were sighted at 1240 hrs directly ahead of us about 8000 ft below. They made a wide circle above a thin overcast at 19,000 ft and went into a string formation and headed down for two ships off Oro Bay, which was ten to fifteen miles away. We dived hard after them once we had dropped our auxiliary tanks, and I gave instructions to attack – "This is our meat".

'My first burst at about 17,000 ft caught a bomber. It lost pieces as my wingman and I passed very close on our way overhead. No 3 man in the flight, Lt [Leonides] Mathers, pulled out to the side and headed for one plane. The second half of the enemy formation seemed to split wide open and they made no attack. However, the first half had apparently scored a hit on one of our vessels as it was smoking badly.

Danny Roberts was a skilled and popular P-38 pilot who claimed his first victories while flying the type as a member of the 80th FS during the defence of the northern New Guinea coast in April 1943

Capt Danny Roberts' first two kills with the 432nd FS/475th FG on 21 August 1943 made him an ace, as he claimed four victories (two flying the P-400 and two in a P-38G) whilst previously serving with the 80th FS/8th FG. CO of the 475th FG's 433rd FS for just 37 days, he turned the underachieving unit around and claimed seven victories in the process. On 9 November Capt Roberts was lost in an operational accident over Alexishafen when he collided with his wingman, 2Lt Dale Meyer, while chasing an 'Oscar' just minutes after claiming another Ki-43 (originally listed erroneously as a 'Hamp') at low altitude for his 14th victory

'At this point three enemy planes flew under me. A sharp turn downwards set me in a position for a good burst, which was fired at one of them at about 5500 ft. A part of its right wing was lost and the dive-bomber immediately made a violent turn, apparently out of control, and headed for the sea, smoking as it went. The plane was seen to strike the sea. My No 3 man then passed under me, with dive-bombers in front of him and fighters on his tail. I dived towards the water to help him, by which time he had destroyed the plane in front of him. It burst into flames and hit the water, burning.'

Roberts claimed two 'Vals' upon returning to base, these successes representing his third and fourth kills – he had destroyed two Zero-sens while flying the P-400 Airacobra in August 1942. He would go on to become a legend in the Fifth Air Force, scoring ten more aerial victories while flying the P-38 before a fatal collision with a squadronmate ended his life on 9 November 1943.

Another pilot with Airacobra kills to his name was 1Lt Don McGee, who had recently joined the 80th FS from the 36th FS. He was at first somewhat unenthusiastic about converting to the 'flying bedstead', as the twin-boomed P-38 was sometimes known. McGee soon changed his mind. His first success with the Lockheed fighter came in an unequal combat during the morning of 12 April, when he led the only three 80th FS fighters to get off the ground for another interception mission.

Approaching Port Moresby at 30,000 ft were 45 'Betty' bombers, escorted by a large number of Zero-sens flying 3000 ft above them. McGee led his three P-38s to attack a group of nine Japanese G4Ms that had descended to 21,000 ft for their bombing runs. He was almost directly overhead Kila airstrip when he made a front quarter attack on a 'Betty'. McGee then pulled up to rake the bomber's belly with two bursts of fire from a range of about 25 yards. McGee was forced to dive away from four of the escorting Zero-sens, but not before he watched the bomber drop out of formation with bullet holes clearly visible from nose to tail. The 'Betty's' demise was later confirmed.

There was an even larger raid on Port Moresby later that same morning, when more than 130 Zero-sens escorted two waves of 'Bettys' intent on blunting the growing Allied air threat based in New Guinea. The fighters involved came from the aircraft carriers *Zuikaku*, *Junyo*, *Hiyo* and *Zuiho*, as well as from the 204th and 582nd Kokutais at Rabaul. Frantic calls went out at 1000 hrs when radar detected large Japanese formations heading for Port Moresby. The 39th FS was duly scrambled to confront the enemy with a small force of about eight P-38s, led by Capt Tom Lynch. Just as the bombers came into view another flight took off a few minutes later, led by Capt Charles Gallup.

About 45 'Bettys' escorted by 60 Zero-sens attacked 5-Mile, 12-Mile and 14-Mile Dromes at Kila, causing moderate damage. Five Japanese aircraft were claimed to have been shot down by 39th pilots, with a 'Zeke' falling to Capt Gallup for his sixth, and last, kill. 1Lt Richard 'Snuffy' Smith claimed a 'Betty' for his third of seven kills, while a second bomber crashed near Mount Chamberlain after 1Lt Dick Suehr attacked it in full view of hundreds of civilian witnesses – this victory was Suehr's fifth, and last, kill.

The 9th FS also managed to get a few P-38s into the battle, one flight claiming five of the Japanese raiders. Future nine-victory ace 2Lt Grover Fanning waded into a heavily-escorted 'Betty' formation to claim two bombers destroyed, and he was also credited with downing an 'Oscar' as well.

Japanese sources do not record any casualties among the escorts, but at least six bombers were lost, with others limping back to base with heavy damage. American records are possibly influenced by the fact that the attack came as something of a surprise, and also that the interceptors were forced to confront the Japanese raiders almost directly over their bases. One indication of the suddenness of the attack is that some of the Zero-sens were identified as 'Oscars'.

Forty-eight hours later another raid again surprised the Allied defenders when a large force of 'Bettys', escorted by Zero-sens from Rabaul, and 'Vals' and Zero-sens from the carriers arrived over Milne Bay. They were met by just three P-38s from the 9th FS, one of which was flown by 1Lt Dick Bong. He claimed a 'Betty' destroyed and a second bomber as a probable. With these victories Bong's tally now stood at ten. The only American loss was 1Lt William Sells, who was killed when he stalled his badly damaged P-38 after pulling up to avoid colliding with an Australian Kittyhawk that had cut in front of him as he attempted to land at the RAAF's Gurney Field. Three 'Bettys' were among the losses reported by Japanese sources.

This attack represented the climax of Operation *I-Go*, which was considered a success by Adm Yamamoto after he received a series of inaccurate and unintentionally exaggerated reports from the aircrews involved that overstated the damage the raids had inflicted. Admittedly,

Capt Charles Gallup achieved early success as a 39th FS/35th FG pilot, claiming six victories and two probables between 27 December 1942 and 12 April 1943. His first kill was achieved in this P-38F-5, 42-12627, when he downed a 'Zeke' over Buna. His remaining victories came in P-38F-5s 42-12621 and 42-12657

the offensive did cause the Allies to be cautious about the enemy's ability to attack its main air and sea bases in New Guinea and the Solomon Islands, but the build up of air power continued nevertheless. Ultimately, however, the perceived success of the offensive resulted in the IJN erroneously withdrawing its aircraft carriers from the theatre after the Japanese believed that the Allied aerial threat in the region had been negated. And, of course, Adm Yamamoto was killed shortly thereafter while travelling to congratulate units that had participated in the operation.

FORTRESS RABAUL

Adm Yamamoto's death marked a turning point in the New Guinea campaign. Fewer raids were suffered by Port Moresby and a greater build-up of Allied air power meant that Japanese bases along the northern coast of New Guinea would inevitably fall. Lae would be invaded in September 1943 and Finschhafen succumbed soon after. Control of the Huon Gulf area was now virtually in Allied hands, and New Britain was within reach of escorted bombing raids. The Japanese fortress of Rabaul could reasonably be neutralised by heavy raids or via the seizure of strategic positions like the Admiralty Islands. In any event, Maj Gen Kenney was clearly on the offensive with his long-ranging Fifth Air Force and its P-38s.

June and July 1943 saw an increase in the number of engagements fought between New Guinea-based P-38s and JAAF fighter units in particular. Dick Bong claimed one 'Oscar' destroyed and a second example damaged over Bena Bena on 12 June. The best day of his first combat tour came on 26 July when he was credited with two more 'Oscars' and a pair of brand new inline-engined Kawasaki Ki-61 'Tonys' in the Markham Valley area to take his score to 15 confirmed victories. Two days later Bong added another 'Oscar' to consolidate his position as the leading American fighter ace in-theatre.

Squadronmate Capt James 'Duckbutt' Watkins also enjoyed success against the Ki-61 on 26 July when he was credited with downing no fewer than four of them. These victories, combined with a solitary Zero-sen kill he had claimed in December 1942 while flying a P-40E, made Watkins an ace. On 28 July he was credited with three 'Oscars' to give him seven P-38 victories. During the clash on the 26th Watkins had had an 'Oscar' shot off his tail by future 22-victory ace 1Lt Gerald 'Johnnie Eager' Johnson, and the men became firm friends afterwards. Johnson had earned his nickname after volunteering for every mission going in an effort to give himself as much opportunity for combat as possible. He was credited with both an 'Oscar' and a 'Tony' destroyed following the 26 July mission.

Johnson was an unusually adept fighter pilot who went from being an air cadet in the summer of 1941 to a full colonel in July 1945. He had a twin brother, Harold, who

Capt James 'Duckbutt' Watkins of the 9th FS/49th FG thought that he was going home with only a single kill to his name as his combat tour neared its end in the late summer of 1943. However, in just three missions between 26 July and 2 August his score rose to 11 kills – hence the smile on his face in this official USAAF photograph, taken in August 1943. Watkins and Jerry Johnson became firm friends during the frenetic action of mid-1943, when the two aces were reputed to have shot an enemy aircraft off each other's tail

NEW GUINEA – THE FIGHTER PILOTS' WAR

37

Capt James Watkins and his P-38G-10 42-12882 were photographed shortly after the former had scored the last kills of his first combat tour in 1943. Watkins claimed a stunning ten victories in three missions in the space of a week – four on 26 July, three on 28 July and three on 2 August

also became a USAAF pilot. 'Johnnie Eager' was also a complete P-38 devotee who once offered to settle an argument with the legendary Thunderbolt ace Neel Kearby to determine the relative value of the P-47 and P-38 in a mock dogfight over Port Moresby. According to legend, fellow P-38-loving pilot Dick Bong actually flew against Kearby. Indeed, an entry in Bong's logbook for 1 August 1943 records the event.

Like the 9th FS, the 80th FS had also seen combat in June 1943 – specifically on the 21st during a routine supply drop escort mission to Guadagasal, a forward base south of Lae. Over Lae itself the P-38s sighted about 30 'Oscars' accompanied by a number of unidentified bombers. Pilots from the 80th immediately engaged the enemy in a wild fight. 2Lt Cornelius 'Corky' Smith was mixing it with the Japanese fighters when he shook an 'Oscar' from his tail by making a steep climb into a cloud. When he looked back just prior to entering the cloud cover he saw 'P-38s and Zeroes all over the sky. All the Zeroes were below me. Several were falling with smoke pouring from them'. Smith subsequently joined up with another P-38 and attacked an 'Oscar' until it fell spinning out of control with part of its wing shot off. A further two Ki-43s fell to Smith's guns for the first three of an eventual 11 victories.

Squadronmate Capt George Welch also enjoyed success on 21 June, having transferred to the 80th FS after scoring three victories while flying P-39s in December 1942 with the unit's sister squadron, the 36th FS. He had been the USAAC's hero at Pearl Harbor when he claimed to have shot down four Japanese raiders while aloft in his P-40B during the infamous 7 December 1941 raid. Welch recounted the 21 June clash in his combat report as follows;

'I dropped tanks and dived on them, starting one smoking, but I didn't see him crash as my right engine cut out due to the fact that the right selector valve wasn't clicked in place. I then lost them and headed to Lae,

2Lts Ken Taylor and George Welch claimed six victories between them when Pearl Harbor was attacked on 7 December 1941. Although Taylor failed to add to his score, 'Wheaties' Welch claimed three more in a P-39D exactly a year later, followed by nine flying P-38G/Hs with the 80th FS/ 8th FG during the summer of 1943. Amongst his Lightning kills were a trio of Ki-61s downed near Wewak on 20 August 1943. Joining North American Aviation as a test pilot in 1944, Welch's post-war career saw him perform the first flights of the P-82 Twin Mustang and F-86 Sabre. He was killed in a crash at Edwards AFB on 12 October 1954 while testing the new F-100 Super Sabre

Capt George Welch was assigned veteran P-38G-15 43-2203 when he switched from the 36th FS to the 80th FS in 1943. This photograph of the aircraft was taken some time between June and August 1943 when the 80th FS was based at Port Moresby. Welch completed an impressive combat career by claiming three 'Zekes' (more likely 'Oscars') and a 'Dinah' on 2 September 1943 whilst flying 43-2203

Future eight-kill ace 2Lt John L Jones of the 80th FS was generally credited with scoring Fifth Fighter Command's 500th aerial victory on 21 May 1943 when he sent a 'Hap' (Zero-sen) down in flames north of Salamaua whilst flying P-38G-15 43-2386 – he got two more kills (both 'Zekes') with it on 21 July. Photographed several months later, Jones is seen here posing with 43-2386, whose scoreboard also denotes victories (13 in total) claimed in it by several other pilots, including aces Cy Homer and Ken Ladd

where I saw eight "Zekes" ["Oscars"] doing acrobatics over the town at 10,000 ft. I dived on them and set one on fire from a head-on pass. He rolled over onto his back and dived into the ocean. I followed through the cloud and saw a "Zeke" ["Oscar"] about 100 ft ahead of me on a course of 90 degrees. He didn't change course, and when I fired half of his wing and fuselage fell off'.

21 July proved to be something of a red-letter day for both the 80th and 39th FSs, with pilots from the former unit claiming 11 victories (1Lt Jay 'Cock' Robbins downed three 'Zekes' and Maj Ed 'Porky' Cragg and 1Lt John Jones each claimed two apiece) and the 39th going one better with 12 kills. These victories meant that the 39th had become the first V Fighter Command squadron to reach 100 confirmed kills. Amongst those making victory claims were Capt Charles King with a single 'Oscar' and 1Lt Paul Stanch with an 'Oscar' and a 'Zeke' to 'make ace'. 1Lt Richard 'Snuffy' Smith also became an ace when he claimed two 'Tonys', while Ken Sparks got an 'Oscar' for his 11th, and final, victory.

August was the month when Maj Gen Kenney's Fifth Air Force went on the offensive, with the Japanese stronghold of Wewak, on the northern coast of New Guinea, being persistently targeted. In turn, the JAAF initially mounted a robust defence against the Allied bombing raids, resulting in more victory claims for the escorting P-38 pilots.

Perhaps the most significant development for the Fifth Air Force was the introduction to combat of the crack P-38-equipped 475th FG. US Army Chief of Staff Gen George Marshall had met Kenney and promised him enough Lightnings to equip an entire group if he could staff it from his own resources. The innovative Kenney managed to scrape together enough pilots and support personnel from his own units as well as other commands and reserve units to bring the new group to life. From within his own squadrons he found future aces such as John Loisel, Verl Jett, Tom McGuire, Harry Brown, Charles MacDonald and Edward Czarnecki, among others. Like the American Volunteer Group (AVG) – better known as the 'Flying Tigers' – the 475th comprised the best and most experienced fighter pilots available. Unsurprisingly, the group immediately started compiling an impressive combat record once declared operational at Dobodura, in New Guinea, on 14 August.

The 475th arrived just in time to participate in the initial assault on Wewak. It immediately set victory records, with pilots claiming 50+ aerial victories in August alone. Leading the way was 1Lt Tom McGuire of the 431st FS, who was an Aleutians veteran. He had also completed three months of combat with the 9th FS/49th FG, prior to joining the 475th. Having failed to make a claim with the 49th, McGuire had downed seven aircraft in three engagements on 18, 21 and 29 August to achieve acedom. Squadronmate Capt Harry Brown, who had claimed a 'Val' during the Pearl Harbor raid while flying a P-36A and an

'Oscar' with the 9th FS in March 1943, was credited with three more Ki-43s over Wewak on 16 August to 'make ace' too.

Many of the claims were certainly exaggerated, but no more so than those of other American units in the area. In one case two P-38 pilots attacked the same 'Oscar' and claimed its destruction three times, even though their foe managed to escape and re-engage the Lightnings before safely landing his damaged machine! In another instance four P-38s attacked a 'twin-engined' fighter and shot it down, even though every post-action report stated that only the reporting pilot had hit the enemy aircraft. Such are the vagaries of observations from excited pilots in stressful situations. Whatever the raw numbers may have been, the American pilots were undoubtedly dominating the aerial battles over Wewak. Indeed, Japanese records viewed after the war indicated a developing respect for the American fighter pilots.

An engagement on 20 August perfectly illustrates the confused nature of victory claiming in this theatre during the war. The 39th FS, whilst escorting bombers to Wewak, intercepted defending 'Oscars' and Kawasaki Ki-45 'Nick' twin-engined fighters from the 13th Sentai. 1Lt Stanley Andrews was flying in his veteran P-38F-5 42-12659 when he claimed a 'Zeke' (it was an 'Oscar', as there were no IJNAF aircraft airborne that day) five miles from Boram strip for his sixth, and final, victory. Minutes earlier Maj Tom Lynch had claimed two 'Nicks' for his ninth and tenth P-38 victories (13 overall). Japanese records state, however, that only one 13th Sentai aircraft failed to return to Rabaul.

Lynch was quite conscientious about his claims, so the question is whether the second 'Nick' actually crashed or was mistakenly listed as definitely shot down. One of the Ki-45s was thought to have crashed about 30 miles south of Wewak. Although based at Rabaul, the 13th Sentai probably operated from Wewak for this interception. It is possible that the second 'Nick' crash-landed near Wewak and was repaired, enabling it to return to Rabaul. The Japanese system of recording losses was sometimes complex, as was the case with most contemporary air arms.

Capt Harry Brown became the 475th FG's first ace when he claimed three Japanese fighters over Wewak while flying this P-38H-1 (42-66592) on 16 August 1943. He had previously claimed a kill during the defence of Pearl Harbor on 7 December 1941, followed by a victory whilst serving with the P-38-equipped 9th FS/49th FG on 4 March 1943. Brown's final success came on 24 October 1943 (*Harry Brown*)

Maj Tom Lynch stands next to his P-38G-1 42-12859 shortly after it had been decorated with a kill decal for his most recent victory – a 'Hamp' downed on the afternoon of 8 May 1943. Lynch had run his tally to 13 by the end of the year

1Lt Ken Ladd and his crew chief TSgt Yale Saffro pose for the camera beside their early P-38H-1 42-66570. Ladd was a popular and aggressive pilot within the 80th FS/8th FG, claiming 12 victories between 23 July 1943 and his death in combat on 14 October 1944 – he claimed two Ki-43s destroyed minutes before he was killed. Ladd achieved only one confirmed success while flying this P-38, downing an 'Oscar' in the Wewak area on 15 September, although he probably continued to use the aircraft until the end of the year (*Yale Saffro via Lex McAulay*)

Aces 1Lt Cy Homer (in P-38G-1 42-12705, coded 'V') and Maj 'Porky' Cragg (in P-38H-1 42-66835) escort B-25D-15 41-30594 of the 501st Bombardment Squadron/345th Bombardment Group as it heads for the Japanese stronghold of Rabaul on 2 November 1943. P-38s escorting B-25s proved a deadly combination. While the Lightnings kept Japanese fighters at bay, ground-strafing Mitchells (and A-20 Havocs) would be free to attack Japanese airfields at low level with devastating results. Cragg claimed a 'Val' and a 'Zeke' probably destroyed during this mission

Following the Wewak offensive, Allied air power turned its attention to the Lae-Salamaua area once again in early September. An American parachute regiment was dropped into the Markham Valley on 1 September, and three days later an amphibious landing was made by the Australian Army's 9th Division near Lae. The latter drew stiff resistance from the air.

Covering the Lae campaign provided new scoring opportunities for the 80th FS, and on 2 September the action was particularly fierce. Flt Off Ed 'de Drunk' DeGraffenreid claimed an 'Oscar' over Wewak to register his fourth of six victories, while the popular 1Lt Ken Ladd scored his second victory when he downed a Mitsubishi Ki-46 'Dinah' reconnaissance aircraft southwest of Madang. The bulk of the day's scoring was attributed to Capt George Welch, however, the 8th FG's operations officer claiming three 'Zekes' (probably 'Oscars') destroyed – two of the fighters collided while attempting to avoid his accurate fire – and another 'Dinah'. These four victories put him level with Dick Bong as the Southwest Pacific's top ace with 16 kills. Flying with the 80th FS that day, he was rotated home shortly thereafter when his tour came to an end.

The price of this success on the 2nd was the loss of 1Lt Bob Adams, who had 'made ace' on 29 August when he downed a 'Zeke' and a 'Nick' over Wewak. Another popular and skilled pilot from the 80th FS, he roamed the New Guinea skies in a resolute mission to hunt down the enemy after he had unsuccessfully attempted to prevent Japanese fighters from strafing a squadronmate hanging helplessly in his parachute. On 2 September Adams was seen chasing an enemy fighter when he simply disappeared, never to return.

The 80th engaged the enemy again on 4 September, when its pilots were called on to defend the Australian amphibious landings from aerial attack. In the vanguard of the action was 1Lt Cyril Homer, who claimed

his fourth victory when he sent a 'Zeke' crashing into the sea east of Salamaua. Maj 'Porky' Cragg was Homer's flight leader on this occasion, and he chased after a Zero-sen that he quickly shot down between Lae and Salamaua. Cragg also saw another member of his flight, 1Lt 'Cock' Robbins, score his fifth victory below him. He was then alarmed to see a number of Zero-sens position themselves between Robbins and the shore, thus cutting off his route to safety.

Diving to his assistance, Cragg shouted a warning to Robbins, who was now trapped out over the sea with a malfunctioning radio. He turned into his attackers and fired desperately as his P-38 took hits in both engines and the cockpit. For several desperate minutes he fought for his life. In fact, he fought so hard that he was to claim three of his assailants shot down and two more damaged. Robbins finally fought his way to the New Guinea coast, and the welcome sight of friendly fighters. By then his P-38 was not only damaged but also out of ammunition. An ashen-faced Robbins returned to base, where an understanding Capt Cragg granted him a few days' leave. He also began the process of confirming the four kills that would boost Robbins' score to seven aerial victories.

1Lt Jay T Robbins of the 80th FS/8th FG used this P-38H-5 (42-66820) to down four 'Zekes' between Lae and Salamaua on 4 September 1943, thus taking his overall score to seven. He claimed his second four-victory haul (all 'Hamps') on 24 October over Rabaul – again in 42-66820. Robbins may also have been flying this P-38 when he gained his final victories of 1943, downing two 'Zekes' over Cape Gloucester on 26 December (*USAF*)

After the fall of Lae and Salamaua in mid September, Finschhafen was next to be targeted. One of the major attributes of the theatre's Allied planners was the speed with which they were able to organise and execute operations against the Japanese. Within days of Lae falling an invasion convoy was steaming toward Finschhafen. 'Betty' bombers returning from a mission discovered the invasion fleet near Cape Cretin during the early evening of 21 September, setting the scene for a classic aerial battle the next day involving, on the Allied side, P-38s, P-40s and P-47s.

A hastily assembled Japanese attack force, comprising eight torpedo-carrying 'Bettys' from the 751st Kokutai, escorted by 23 Zero-sens of the 253rd Kokutai and at least 15 more fighters from the 201st and

1Lt Jay T Robbins of the 80th FS/8th FG was photographed in the cockpit of his P-38H-5 42-66820 sometime between the missions on 21 July and 4 September 1943. He accounted for seven 'Zekes' destroyed and three more as probables on these dates. The four victories and two probables credited to him on 4 September were claimed in this aircraft

1Lt John Lane and Capt Paul Stanch of the 39th FS/35th FG are seen with Lane's P-38F-5 42-12644 in late August 1943. Lane had scored his sixth, and last, victory by this time, while Stanch, who also had six kills to his name, would take his final tally to ten during the Rabaul operations in October (*USAF*)

Future ten-kill ace 2Lt Elliott Summer of the 432nd FS/475th FG strikes a pose in a rarely seen flying jacket during his time with the group in Queensland in July 1943. Such thick apparel was only appropriate for winter flying in Australia, and had no place in the hot and humid weather of the Southwest Pacific

204th Kokutais, was despatched from Rabaul against the convoy. The 'Bettys' took off at 0840 hrs in three waves, the first being led by Lt(jg) Yada, the second led by NCO Jitsuyoshi Kuramasu, and the last two aircraft by CPO Aoki. Cheering crews on the ground waved their hats as the bombers circled the field before heading down the length of New Britain toward the landing beaches at Finschhafen. Although 20 Zero-sens took up position above and behind the bombers, the 'Betty' crews knew that their chances of surviving a daylight torpedo attack were not high.

Landings on Scarlet beach, near the Song River just north of Finschhafen, had started at 0445 hrs on 22 September. Australian troops made swift progress inland, quickly capturing the town's key airstrip. American air attacks against the enemy's defensive installations in the area continued, with what were considered to be good results despite cloud.

Around noon fighter directors aboard the destroyer USS *Reid* (DD-369) started to see a large number of radar returns less than 70 miles from the now retiring Finschhafen convoy, which had safely offloaded the invasion force. The aircraft were inbound from New Britain. Although the three USAAF fighter squadrons (the 341st with P-47s, the P-40-equipped 35th and the 39th with P-38s) that had been protecting the convoy were due for relief just minutes after the IJNAF formation was spotted, all aircraft still had sufficient fuel to engage the approaching enemy force.

At 1245 hrs near the island of Tami, some 30 miles off Finschafen, six P-38s engaged the escorting Zero-sens. They claimed seven of the Japanese fighters destroyed, including one downed inadvertently by ramming. This resulted in the day's only loss, suffered by the 39th, when Lt Forest went down with his stricken aircraft. Capt Charles King erroneously claimed an 'Oscar' destroyed (and a second as a probable) for his third victory, 'Snuffy' Smith downed a 'Zeke' (and claimed a second one as damaged) for his seventh, and final, victory of his tour, and Capt Paul Stanch accounted for two more Zero-sens to take his tally to nine confirmed victories.

The 475th FG's 432nd FS was also involved in the action on 22 September, its pilots setting a single mission record for the theatre by claiming to have shot down seven 'Bettys' and eleven Zero-sens after they intercepted the IJNAF force between 1240 hrs and 1250 hrs. Capt Fred 'Squareloop' Harris was credited with the biggest haul, claiming two 'Zekes' and a 'Betty' to 'make ace'. Future aces 1Lts James Ince and Vivian Cloud and 2Lt Zach Dean each accounted for a 'Betty' and a 'Zeke'. Cloud had to abandon his P-38 shortly thereafter, although he was soon rescued by a destroyer. His wingman, 2Lt Donald Garrison, was also shot down, and he did not return.

The final claims at day's end totalled nine 'Bettys' and approximately 29 Zerosens, divided between four fighter squadrons and anti-aircraft gun crews aboard vessels in the convoy.

Another Japanese fighter had also been claimed in the area that day when the 433rd FS's Capt Joe McKeon downed a 'Tony' shortly before the main battle commenced.

Japanese records state that eight 'Bettys' and a similar number of Zerosens had been lost. One of the bombers was destroyed in a crash landing at Rabaul when Jitsuyoshi Kuramasu managed to get his badly damaged aircraft home. The large number of American fighters participating in the engagement, as well as confusion caused by anti-aircraft fire from the ships they were protecting, tended to obscure the results of the battle. Whatever the final count, there is no doubt that the Japanese had suffered a major defeat when the convoy was allowed to retire virtually intact. The cost to the Americans included three P-38s and a P-40 destroyed. Depending on sources, Japanese aircraft losses ranged from 16 up to 40.

This photograph of 1Lt 'Frank' Lent posing with his P-38H-1 42-66550 was taken in late October 1943. His score officially stood at seven at the time, but some enterprising soul scratched four more victory flags onto this print after Lent claimed his final kills in March 1944!

RABAUL UNDER SIEGE

With the Huon peninsula coming under Allied control, together with islands like Woodlark and Kiriwina, the possibility of escorted bombing raids on the Rabaul area became a reality. The decision not to invade the fortress itself meant taking territory as close to New Britain as possible, with such advances being closely supported by aerial bombardment from New Guinea, the Solomon Islands and aircraft carriers at sea. Maj Gen Kenney was the first off the mark when he gathered enough B-24s, B-25s and P-38s to sustain a substantial bombing campaign against Rabaul. Manus Island, in the Admiralties, would be taken in early 1944 and the islands of the Solomons chain closest to New Britain occupied to further isolate Rabaul.

The first attack from the New Guinea area was mounted on 12 October when a large force of B-24s and B-25s, covered by all available P-38s, apparently took the Japanese by surprise. Many aircraft were claimed to have been destroyed on the ground at Tobera and Kokopo, as well as at the main IJNAF base at Vunakanau. A 'Betty' was also shot down by the P-38 escort force. Much damage was done to docks and shore installations, fuel dumps and four ships. There was even a claim that an 'Oscar' had been shot down, despite the fact that no JAAF units were based at Rabaul. Japanese sources specify that nine 'Bettys' were set on fire and more than 30 others sustained significant damage.

Such effrontery would not be tolerated by the enemy for long. At 0830 hrs on 15 October, 15 'Vals' of the 204th Kokutai, led by Lt Ikeda, escorted by 39 Zero-

The four great aces of the 475th FG had already scored heavily by the end of 1943. They are, from left to right, 1Lt Frank Lent, Capt Tom McGuire, Lt Col Charles MacDonald and Capt John Loisel. Between them they had claimed 40 enemy aircraft destroyed during 1943 alone

Enjoying a cigar after 'making ace' over Rabaul on 24 October 1943, 1Lt John 'Jump' O'Neill of the 9th FS/ 49th FG smiles for the camera while sitting in P-38G-13 43-2204 at Dobodura. He had flown Lightnings alongside Dick Bong in California prior to their deployment to the Pacific, and had looped the Golden Gate Bridge on the eve of heading into combat. Bong got the blame for that particular prank

1Lt John O'Neill's P-38G-13 43-2204 boasted both evocative nose art and eight victory symbols after he claimed his final kills over Vunakanau on 29 October 1943 (*John O'Neill*)

sens of the 204th Kokutai, led by WO Aoki, left Rabaul to make a surprise attack on shipping crowded in Oro Bay and, it was hoped, strike a major blow to the Allied campaign. A wild aerial battle ensued in which P-38s of the 9th FS reported engaging 'Vals' and 'Oscars'. Although the combination of types seems unlikely, Capt Jerry Johnson claimed two of the dive-bombers and one of the fighters to take his tally to six victories. 1Lt Grover Fanning also claimed an 'Oscar' for his seventh kill.

The 432nd FS also had another big day, with its pilots claiming 12 victories. Amongst those enjoying success was Capt John Loisel, who claimed to have downed two 'Zekes' in the savage fighting to give him ace status. He and his wingman, 2Lt James Farris, were then forced to perform a series of violent evasive manoeuvres in order to shake off more enemy fighters, before heading home. Fellow ace Capt Fred Harris destroyed two 'Vals' to take his tally to seven, while future aces 1Lts Elliott Summer, Vivian Cloud and 2Lt Billy Gresham all added to their victory scores.

The 431st FS claimed to have shot down 11 enemy aircraft during the same action. 1Lt Tom McGuire added a 'Val' to his tally for his tenth victory to make him the leading ace of the 475th FG, while 2Lt Frank Lent claimed two 'Zekes' and a 'Val' to achieve acedom. 1Lt Ed Czarnecki got a Zero-sen for his fourth victory, while 1Lt Paul Morriss and 2Lts Vince Elliott and Frank Monk all added victories to see them on their way to becoming aces. The 431st's 1Lt Marion Kirby also achieved his first victory, the future ace being so excited during the combat that he held down his firing buttons until the gun barrels warped with the heat and sent tracers off in random directions, rather than converging on the doomed 'Val'.

Pilots from the 433rd FS claimed eight victories, with 2Lt John Smith claiming an enemy fighter for the second of his eventual six victories. Four 'Vals' were also credited to group headquarters pilots, with future CO Maj Charles MacDonald shooting down a pair of 'Vals' for the first of his 27 victories. His fighter had been hit by return fire from one of the dive-bombers during the engagement, and he was forced to nurse his damaged 433rd FS P-38 back to Dobodura and crash-land.

The day's totals amounted to nearly 30 'Vals' and a large number of fighters claimed for the loss of a single P-38. Actual Japanese losses amounted to 14 'Vals' and five Zero-sens, including that of escort leader Aoki. Again, whether the score was 40-to-1 or 19-to-1, it still represented a major defeat for the Japanese. It was also another clear victory for the Lightning.

Two days later (17 October) the Japanese tried again with a strike on the Buna area. This time P-38s of the 9th, 431st and 433rd FSs encountered a force of Zero-sens (possibly from the 204th Kokutai, based at Rabaul) and claimed to have shot down more than

20 enemy fighters for the loss of three Lightnings. The 9th FS's 1Lt Grover Fanning claimed a 'Zeke' and a 'Tony' to take his final score to nine, while squadronmates 1Lts John 'Jump' O'Neill and Ralph Wandrey each added a 'Zeke' to their tallies.

Nine Zero-sens fell to the 431st, three of them to 1Lt Tom McGuire, who then had to bail out of his blazing P-38H-5 42-66836 over Oro Bay with multiple wounds. 1Lt Ed Czarnecki accounted for two 'Zekes' to 'make ace', while 1Lt Marion Kirby and 2Lt Vince Elliott each added a 'Zeke' to their growing tallies. The 433rd claimed ten Zero-sens destroyed, two of them attributed to future ace 2Lt Jack Fisk, two more to Capt Danny Roberts (taking his tally to nine) and a further pair to 2Lt John

Smith, who now had four of his six victories. It was an impressive indication of Danny Roberts' charismatic leadership that the 433rd FS was surging up the victory lists only 14 days after he had taken command of the squadron. More success would follow in the weeks before his loss in combat.

Weather had been as much an enemy as the Japanese during the final months of 1943, cancelling many of the scheduled operations against Rabaul. October had brought the start of the rainy season, with its unpredictable and violent changes of weather. This meant that the next scoring opportunity for the P-38 squadrons would not arrive until 23 October when, during an attack by high-altitude B-24s, escorting P-38 pilots claimed to have shot down around 20 enemy aircraft – a total revised down from an estimated 30+. Capt Paul Stanch of the 39th FS claimed an 'Oscar' for his tenth, and final, victory, while the 475th FG's Maj Charles MacDonald also downed a Ki-43 for his third. 431st FS pilot 2Lt Vince Elliott 'made ace' with claims for a 'Zeke' and a 'Hamp', while squadronmates 1Lts Marion Kirby and Lowell Lutton each got a Mitsubishi fighter to set them on their way to becoming P-38 aces. Finally, Capt 'Johnnie Eager' Johnson of the 9th FS claimed his seventh victory when he downed a 'Zeke'.

A low-level attack on Rabaul by B-25s the following day saw pilots of the 80th FS claim no fewer than 12 victories over the battleground of Kabanga Bay, Rabaul. 1Lt 'Cock' Robbins achieved the extraordinary feat of scoring a second quartet of victories (four 'Hamps', plus a fifth as a probable) in a single mission that day, while Maj Ed Cragg added two more 'Hamps' to his score. Both men now had 11 victories to their names. Former P-70 nightfighter pilot 1Lt Burnell Adams got a 'Hamp' for first kill with the P-38 (he had claimed a 'Sally' bomber with the 6th NFS five months earlier), while 1Lt 'Corky' Smith's 'Zeke' victory gave him ace status.

Despite bad weather on the 25th Maj Charles MacDonald decided to lead his two flights from the 432nd FS as escorts for B-24s targeting Rabaul. By weaving his flights high over the bombers he not only added to their safety but also claimed to have shot down a 'Zeke' that came too close to the American formation. MacDonald's was the sole victory credited to the Allies that day, although Japanese records state that two Zero-sens failed to return from the interception.

The weather was too bad for further escort missions on Rabaul until 29 October, when a major high-altitude raid was mounted by B-24s

Capt Charlie King, pictured here in July 1943, made his first confirmed kill with the 39th FS/35th FG on 2 March 1943 during the opening stages of the Bismarck Sea operation. He 'made ace' on 29 October that same year. A career officer, King also saw combat in the Korean War, flying 66 sorties with the F-86-equipped 4th Fighter Interceptor Wing and claiming a solitary MiG-15 damaged (*Charlie King*)

Nicknamed 'Johnnie Eager', Capt Jerry Johnson of the 9th FS/49th FG earned this sobriquet for the way he 'waded' into Japanese formations with utter fearlessness. He and his combat-weary P-38F-5 (probably 42-12655) were photographed at Dobodura in late October 1943

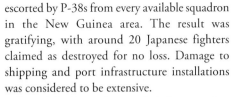

SSgt John Stolarz was the crew chief on P-38G-13 43-2386, which bore the name *'G.I. ANNIE'* on its right side and *'LIL-DE-ICER'* on the left side. The artwork on either side of the fighter's nose was based on publicity photographs of movie star Frances Rafferty. John Jones claimed three of his eight victories in this aircraft, which was eventually lost, along with its pilot, in bad weather over St George's Channel, near New Britain, on 7 November 1943 (*Krane Files*)

A pensive Capt Dick Bong poses with his P-38H-5 42-66847, which was issued to him as a replacement for the Lightning that he had written off on 6 September 1943. This photograph was taken at the end of the Rabaul offensive in November 1943, at which point Bong's tally stood at 21 – he had claimed his final kills of 1943 on 5 November (two 'Zekes' over Rabaul) in 42-66847

escorted by P-38s from every available squadron in the New Guinea area. The result was gratifying, with around 20 Japanese fighters claimed as destroyed for no loss. Damage to shipping and port infrastructure installations was considered to be extensive.

Several P-38 aces increased their scores that day, including Capt Dick Bong, whose two 'Zeke' kills took his tally to 19. Capt Danny Roberts's 'Zeke' was his 11th kill in a P-38 and 13th overall, while squadronmate 2Lt John Smith recorded his sixth, and last, victory when he too downed a 'Zeke'. Both 1Lt Ralph Wandrey of the 9th FS and Maj Charlie King, CO of the 39th FS, 'made ace' with their victories, the former claiming a 'Zeke' while flying a veteran P-38F-5 and the latter getting a 'Zeke' and an 'Oscar' for his final kills.

King had some colour film loaded into the gun camera fitted to his P-38H-5 42-66822, and the footage obtained was spectacular. However, a senior administrative officer failed to keep his promise to return a copy of the film for King's personal use. A mild-mannered soul who seemed never to hold a grudge or make a move in anger, King was a different character in combat. His groundcrews were always impressed by the fierce expression on his face when he climbed from his P-38 after an engagement with the enemy. King's post-action report following the 29 October mission reflects his combat mentality;

'Leading Outcast squadron [the 39th's call-sign], I started into the target area on a fighter sweep approximately five minutes ahead of the bombers. Starting at 26,000 ft, we dropped to 23,000 ft as we crossed Tobera and headed for Vunakanau. Over Vunakanau I saw approximately 20 single-seat fighters to the east at approximately the same level. Pulling up with excess speed, I turned in behind them and executed an attack on the last group of four to five aeroplanes. One made a gentle right turn and I followed him, shooting several bursts in a dive of 15 to 20 degrees and, finally, in a shallow climb. I closed to within 30 yards and saw my bullets tear a hole in the trailing edge of the right wing root about three feet in diameter. He went into a spin and crashed.

'I pulled up into a climb and turned back into the fight, making a couple of passes at enemy fighters with nil visible results and one in which I saw explosive rounds hitting one in the wing. One of them did a snap roll right in front of me as I closed on him. On about my fifth pass I followed one through a slight dive and climb. When I closed to about 100 ft he started what looked like a barrel roll. As I passed over him he was upside down. The bottom of the ship below the cockpit burst into flames. When I last saw it the whole ship seemed to be burning and going down.

'My last pass was at a single-seat fighter that came from ten degrees high. I pulled into a head-on pass. My guns fired about ten rounds and I was out of ammo, so I dived down under him.

47

'I claim one "Zeke" and one "Oscar" destroyed.'

It was determined that the most effective operation against shipping at Rabaul was the standard masthead-height type of raid that had routed the Lae convoys. On 2 November 1943, with the most sanguine expectations that the Japanese fighter force had been significantly reduced, Maj Gen Kenney ordered an audacious attack that backfired badly. The day became known as 'Bloody Tuesday' for the heavy losses incurred by the attacking American aircraft. At least

eight B-25s and nine P-38s were lost in return for claims of about 40 Japanese fighters destroyed. According to IJNAF sources 18 to 20 Zero-sens and possibly one or two JAAF 'Oscars' and 'Tonys' were actually lost. Japanese claims totalled around 90 P-38s, yet the entire force of twin-engined fighters in action over Rabaul that day only amounted to 64!

Claims for seven aircraft shot down were made by 80th FS pilots. They included one by 2Lt Ed DeGraffenreid for his sixth, and last, victory, two for 2Lt Allen Hill (his third and fourth of nine victories) and one for 1Lt John Jones, which proved to be the last of his eight victories. Capt 'Johnnie Eager' Johnson of the 9th FS achieved his eighth and ninth kills, while 1Lt Grover Gholson of the 432nd FS gained two victories to take his score to five, four of which he had achieved in the P-38 (he had claimed a Zero-sen while flying P-39s with the 36th FS in May 1942).

Although the 431st FS made most of the day's claims, it suffered the greatest losses. 1Lt Marion Kirby was credited with two 'Zekes' to take his tally to five, including one piloted by the ace Yoshio Fukui, who parachuted into the harbour. Fukui survived this ordeal to be credited with shooting down 11 American aircraft. 2Lt Frank Lent had shot down another 'Zeke' and then watched Kirby save a B-25 under attack by Fukui. Future ace 2Lt Fred Champlin also claimed two 'Zekes' for his third and fourth victories, while 2Lt Frank Monk got the second of his eventual five kills.

Another to score his fifth victory on this operation was 1Lt Lowell Lutton, who was subsequently posted among the missing at the end of the mission. He was flying on Capt Arthur Wenige's wing coming out of Rabaul. Wenige had also just 'made ace' by claiming two 'Zekes' destroyed (he had a Zero-sen kill from his time flying P-40s with the 9th FS in 1942), and on the way back to Kiriwina he looked behind to see that Lutton was no longer in sight. It is believed that the latter pilot might have run out of fuel in P-38H-5 42-66821.

The next Lightning-escorted raid on Rabaul was flown two days later. Capt Dick Bong claimed two more 'Zekes' to take his total score to 21, the high-scoring ace reporting that the two Japanese fighters were alone and seemed well worn, with bare aluminium showing through their weathered camouflage. Once again Japanese records acknowledge the loss of two fighters to confirm Bong's claims – the only ones made by the Fifth Air Force that day. Bong was now the top-scoring USAAF ace, and Maj Gen Kenney had promised him that when he reached 20 victories he would send Bong on 60 days leave in time for the hunting season in his native Wisconsin. Bong would return twice to the Southwest Pacific in 1944 to claim 19 more victories, making him the all-time high-scoring American ace with 40 kills.

But there were unhappy events in store for the P-38 aces as the Rabaul missions were drawing to a close. On 9 November Capt Danny Roberts was lost in an operational accident over Alexishafen when he collided with his wingman, 2Lt Dale Meyer, while chasing an 'Oscar' just minutes after claiming another Ki-43 (originally listed erroneously as a 'Hamp') at low altitude for his 14th victory. 433rd FS ace 2Lt John Smith was also killed in this action when he was shot down by an enemy fighter.

The last P-38 ace to lose his life in the Southwest Pacific in 1943 was 80th FS CO Maj Ed 'Porky' Cragg, who was reported missing in the Cape Gloucester area shortly after he was observed scoring his 15th victory. That same day the irrepressible Capt Tom McGuire returned to his scoring ways following his recovery from wounds suffered on 17 October. Also engaging the enemy over Cape Gloucester, he waded into a formation of 'Vals' and claimed three of the dive-bombers destroyed to take his score to 16 confirmed victories. He was now the ranking P-38 ace still active in-theatre.

Maj Gen Kenney found that his staunch support for the P-38 as the key offensive fighter in the Southwest Pacific had been vindicated over Rabaul. Yet despite its success, he had gained a new respect for the enemy's endurance and capabilities following the dogged IJNAF and JAAF defence of Japanese-held territory. The losses suffered by V Fighter Command in late 1943 in particular made Kenney more realistic about the pace and strength of the Fifth Air Force's efforts.

The Rabaul campaign also brought other consequences. Various sources put P-38 losses over Rabaul from 12 October to 11 November at between 16 and 22 aircraft. With the worldwide demand for P-38s at its peak by the end of 1943, Kenney was forced to temporarily convert the 9th and 39th FSs to the more abundant P-47D, despite the protests of commanders and pilots alike. For the rest of the year, and into 1944, virtually half of V Fighter Command would be equipped with Republic's portly fighter. This thorny issue would not be fully addressed until mid-1944, when the UK-based Eighth Air Force reined in its voracious appetite for the P-38 in favour of Merlin-engined P-51 Mustangs. Eventually the Fifth Air Force was equipped with three P-38 groups, two flying the P-51 and one equipped with P-47s.

However, it was the Lightning that had been the weapon of choice when battle was joined in the Pacific in 1942 and 1943, and it would continue to be the most favoured equipment in-theatre until war's end.

Maj Edward 'Porky' Cragg commanded the 80th FS/8th FG from March 1943 until he perished in combat on 26 December 1943 over Cape Gloucester. His tally stood at 15 victories at the time of his death, making him the highest-scoring Lightning ace to be killed in 1943. Cragg is stood in front of P-38H-1 42-66506, which he used to claim nine of his victories. He was also lost in this machine

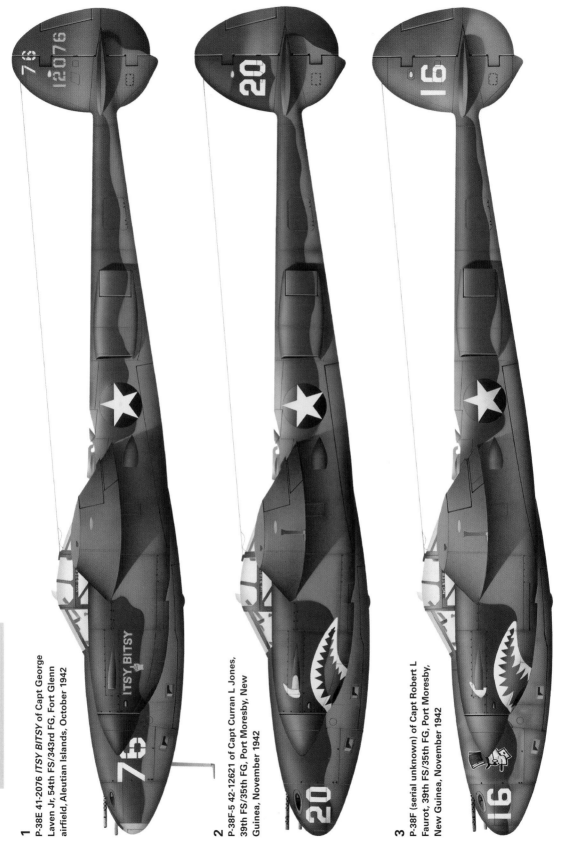

COLOUR PLATES

1
P-38E 41-2076 *ITSY BITSY* of Capt George Laven Jr, 54th FS/343rd FG, Fort Glenn airfield, Aleutian Islands, October 1942

2
P-38F-5 42-12621 of Capt Curran L Jones, 39th FS/35th FG, Port Moresby, New Guinea, November 1942

3
P-38F (serial unknown) of Capt Robert L Faurot, 39th FS/35th FG, Port Moresby, New Guinea, November 1942

50

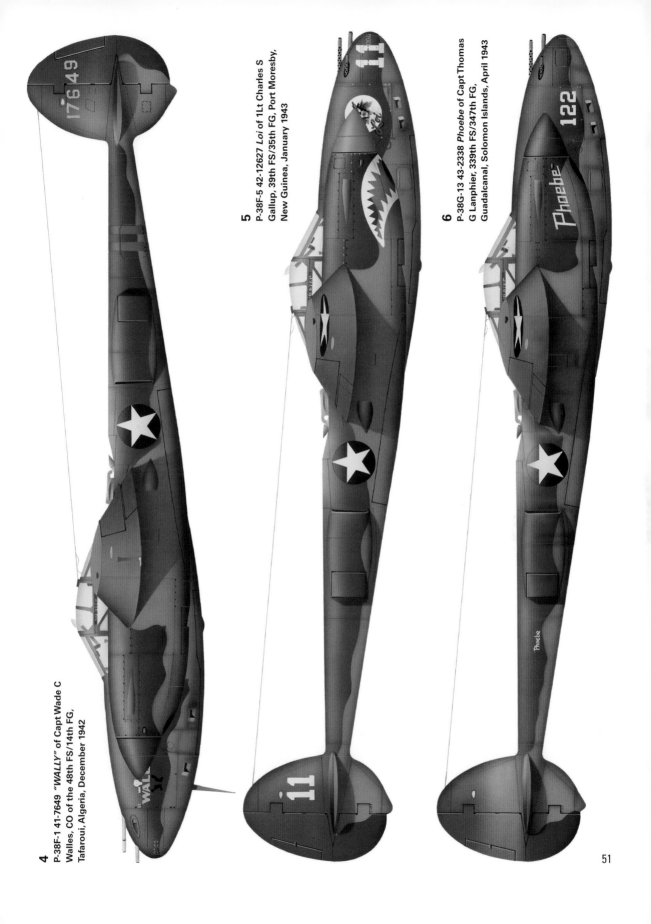

4
P-38F-1 41-7649 "WALLY" of Capt Wade C
Walles, CO of the 48th FS/14th FG,
Tafaroui, Algeria, December 1942

5
P-38F-5 42-12627 *Loi* of 1Lt Charles S
Gallup, 39th FS/35th FG, Port Moresby,
New Guinea, January 1943

6
P-38G-13 43-2338 *Phoebe* of Capt Thomas
G Lanphier, 339th FS/347th FG,
Guadalcanal, Solomon Islands, April 1943

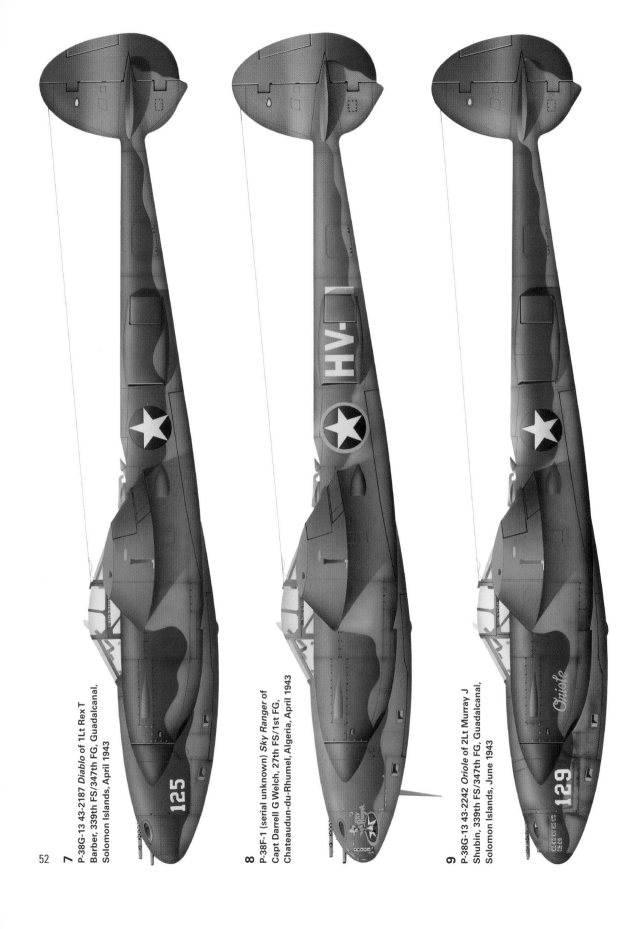

7
P-38G-13 43-2187 *Diablo* of 1Lt Rex T
Barber, 339th FS/347th FG, Guadalcanal,
Solomon Islands, April 1943

8
P-38F-1 (serial unknown) *Sky Ranger* of
Capt Darrell G Welch, 27th FS/1st FG,
Chateaudun-du-Rhumel, Algeria, April 1943

9
P-38G-13 43-2242 *Oriole* of 2Lt Murray J
Shubin, 339th FS/347th FG, Guadalcanal,
Solomon Islands, June 1943

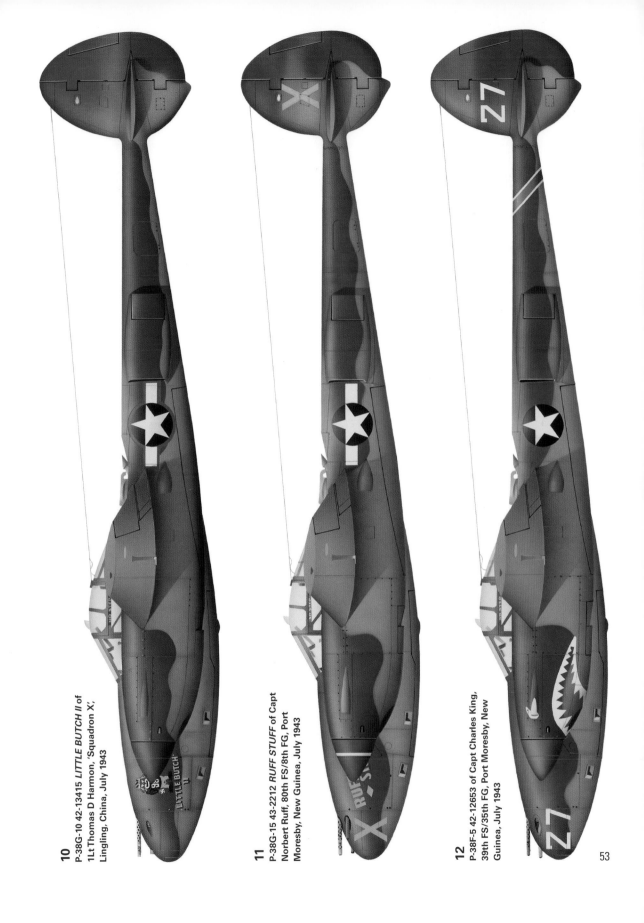

10
P-38G-10 42-13415 *LITTLE BUTCH II* of
1Lt Thomas D Harmon, 'Squadron X',
Lingling, China, July 1943

11
P-38G-15 43-2212 *RUFF STUFF* of Capt
Norbert Ruff, 80th FS/8th FG, Port
Moresby, New Guinea, July 1943

12
P-38F-5 42-12653 of Capt Charles King,
39th FS/35th FG, Port Moresby, New
Guinea, July 1943

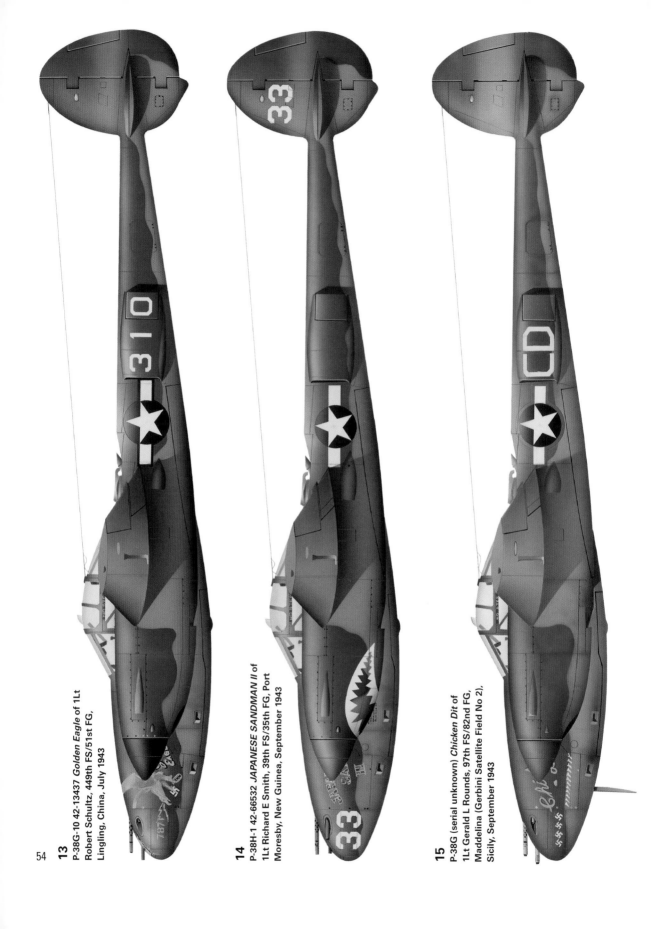

13
P-38G-10 42-13437 *Golden Eagle* of 1Lt
Robert Schultz, 449th FS/51st FG,
Lingling, China, July 1943

14
P-38H-1 42-66532 *JAPANESE SANDMAN II* of
1Lt Richard E Smith, 39th FS/35th FG, Port
Moresby, New Guinea, September 1943

15
P-38G (serial unknown) *Chicken Dit* of
1Lt Gerald L Rounds, 97th FS/82nd FG,
Maddelina (Gerbini Satellite Field No 2),
Sicily, September 1943

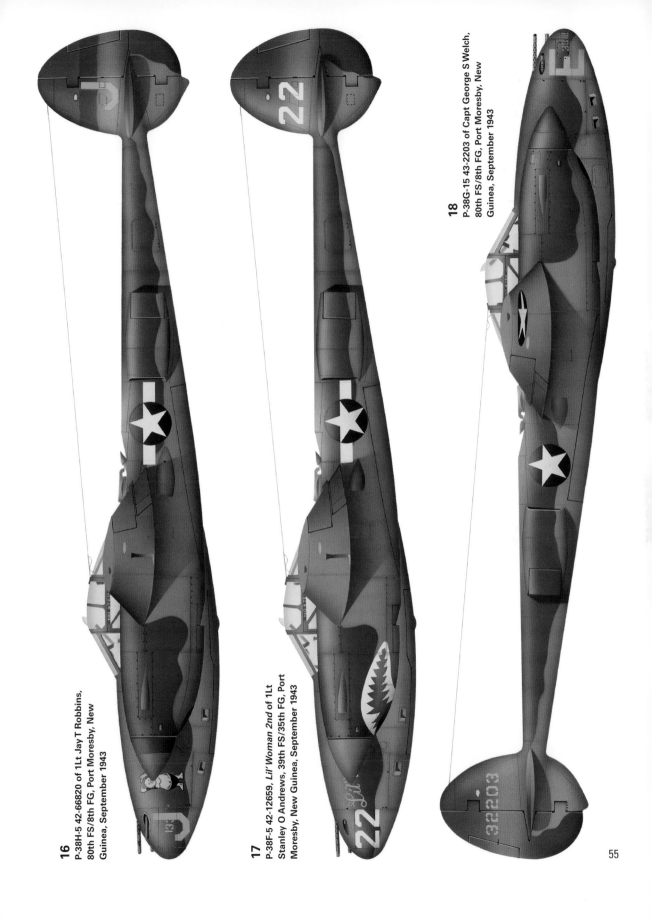

16
P-38H-5 42-66820 of 1Lt Jay T Robbins, 80th FS/8th FG, Port Moresby, New Guinea, September 1943

17
P-38F-5 42-12659, *Lil' Woman 2nd* of 1Lt Stanley O Andrews, 39th FS/35th FG, Port Moresby, New Guinea, September 1943

18
P-38G-15 43-2203 of Capt George S Welch, 80th FS/8th FG, Port Moresby, New Guinea, September 1943

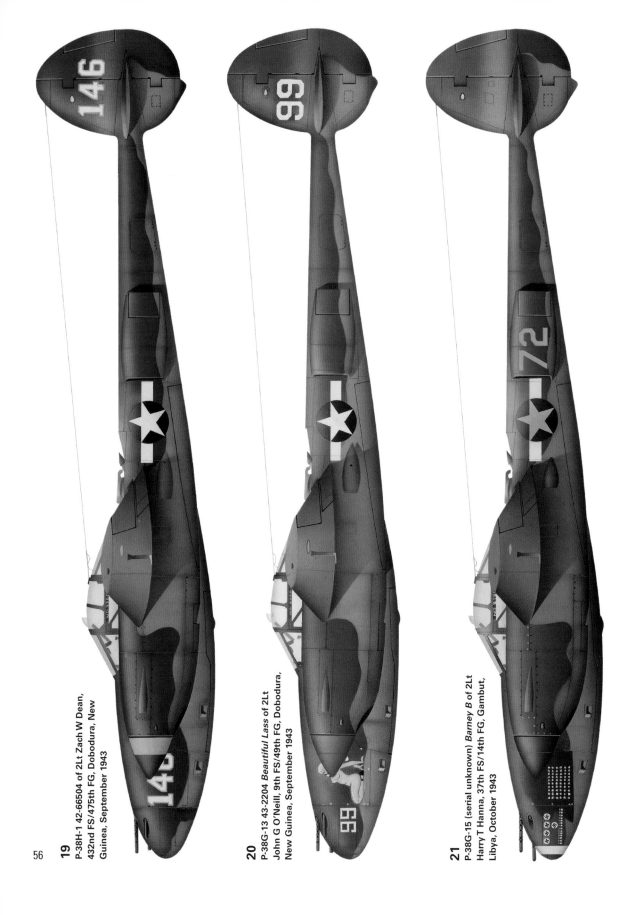

19
P-38H-1 42-66504 of 2Lt Zach W Dean, 432nd FS/475th FG, Dobodura, New Guinea, September 1943

20
P-38G-13 43-2204 *Beautiful Lass* of 2Lt John G O'Neill, 9th FS/49th FG, Dobodura, New Guinea, September 1943

21
P-38G-15 (serial unknown) *Barney B* of 2Lt Harry T Hanna, 37th FS/14th FG, Gambut, Libya, October 1943

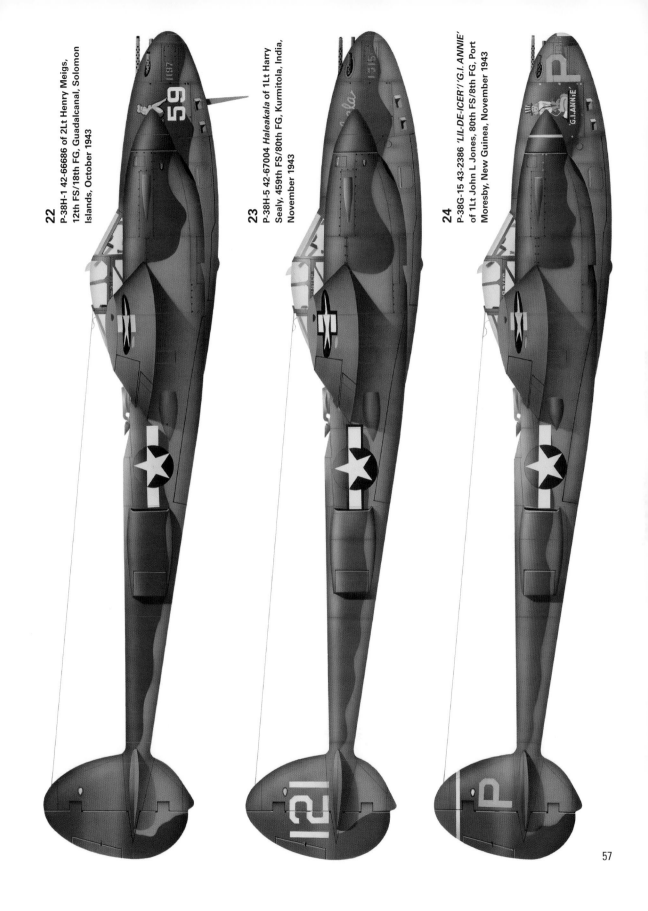

22
P-38H-1 42-66686 of 2Lt Henry Meigs,
12th FS/18th FG, Guadalcanal, Solomon
Islands, October 1943

23
P-38H-5 42-67004 *Haleakala* of 1Lt Harry
Sealy, 459th FS/80th FG, Kurmitola, India,
November 1943

24
P-38G-15 43-2386 'LIL-DE-ICER'/'G.I. ANNIE'
of 1Lt John L Jones, 80th FS/8th FG, Port
Moresby, New Guinea, November 1943

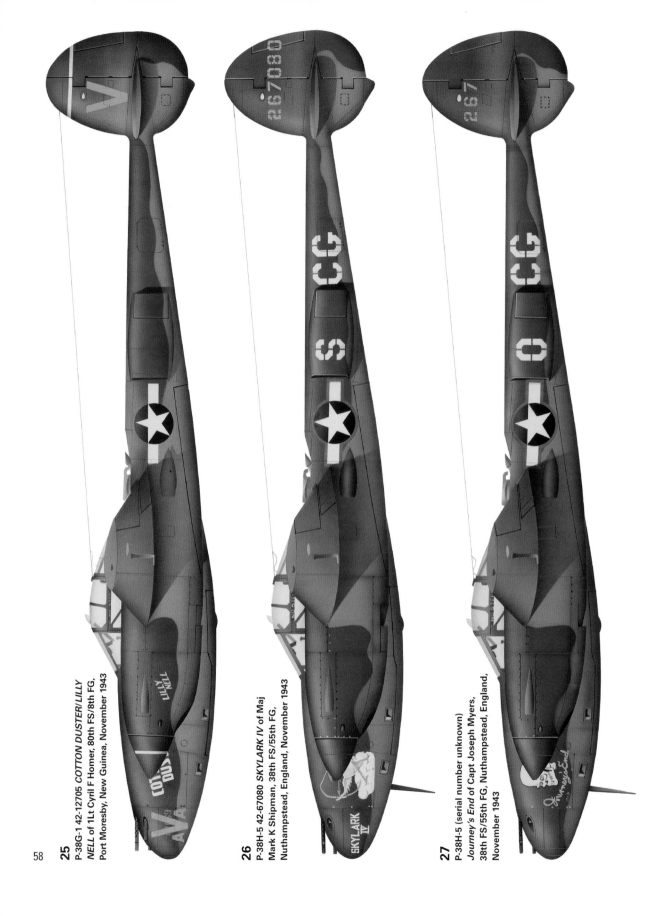

58

25
P-38G-1 42-12705 *COTTON DUSTER/ LILLY*
NELL of 1Lt Cyril F Homer, 80th FS/8th FG,
Port Moresby, New Guinea, November 1943

26
P-38H-5 42-67080 *SKYLARK IV* of Maj
Mark K Shipman, 38th FS/55th FG,
Nuthampstead, England, November 1943

27
P-38H-5 (serial number unknown)
Journey's End of Capt Joseph Myers,
38th FS/55th FG, Nuthampstead, England,
November 1943

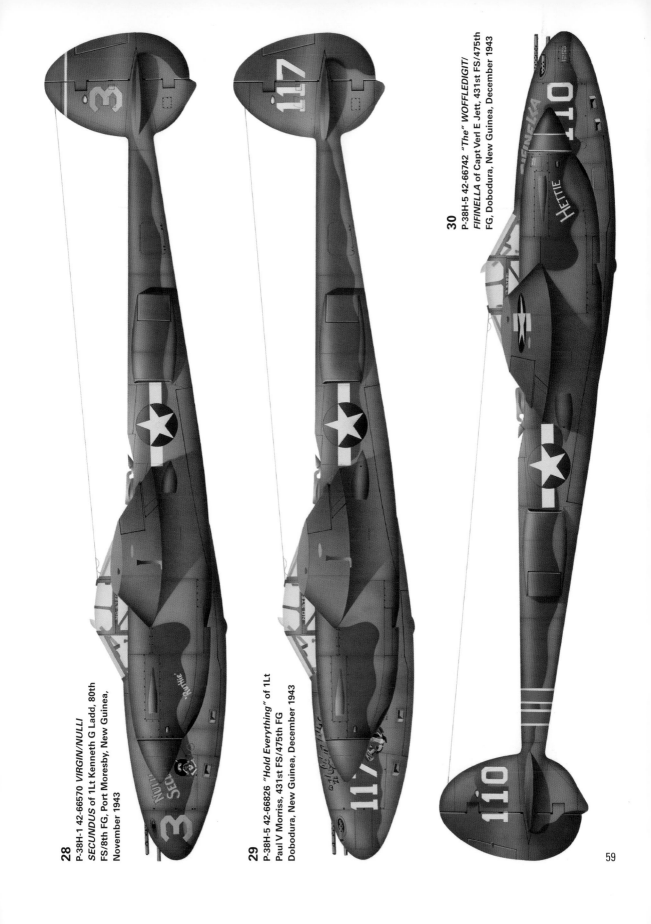

28
P-38H-1 42-66570 *VIRGIN/NULLI
SECUNDUS* of 1Lt Kenneth G Ladd, 80th
FS/8th FG, Port Moresby, New Guinea,
November 1943

29
P-38H-5 42-66826 *"Hold Everything"* of 1Lt
Paul V Morriss, 431st FS/475th FG
Dobodura, New Guinea, December 1943

30
P-38H-5 42-66742 *"The" WOFFLEDIGIT/
FIFINELLA* of Capt Verl E Jett, 431st FS/475th
FG, Dobodura, New Guinea, December 1943

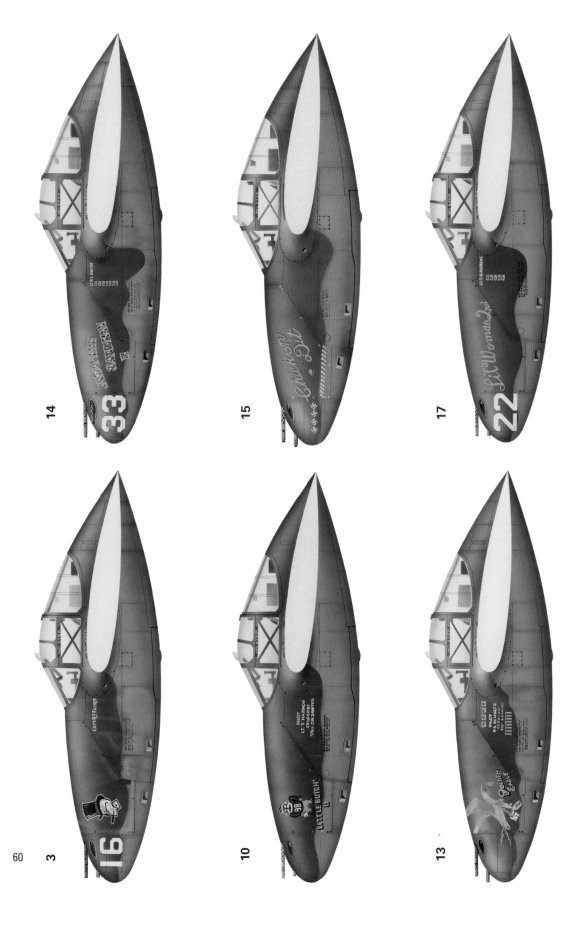

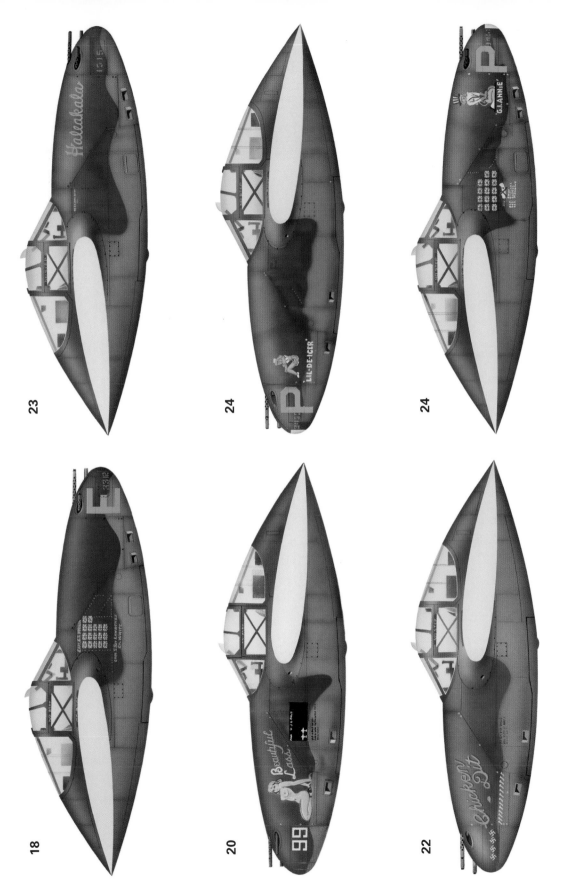

23

24

24

18

20

22

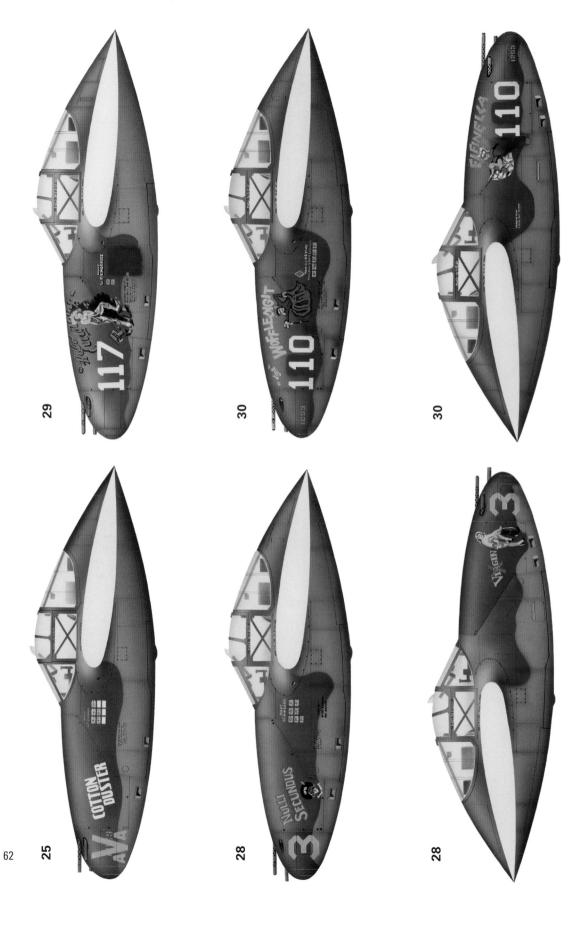

25

29

28

30

28

30

TWIN-TAILED DRAGONS OF THE CBI

Not until mid-summer 1943, when there were enough P-38Gs in North Africa to keep up with heavy combat attrition, were there sufficient Lightnings available to form the first unit scheduled for operations on the China-Burma-India (CBI) front. And it fell to a veteran of the North African campaign to bring together a handful of seasoned twin-engined pilots – mostly men who had flown B-25s, photo-reconnaissance types or P-38s in North Africa – to form a new squadron that would travel east from Morocco to Kunming, China. That man was near-ace Maj Bob Kirtley, who had claimed the first Luftwaffe aircraft shot down by the 82nd FG during the group's over-water flight from England to North Africa in December 1942. He went on to become one of the group's brightest P-38 stars, being credited with four aerial victories and a handful of damaged and probable claims.

For security reasons Kirtley's new unit would be identified as 'Squadron X', and it had joined Lt Gen Claire Chennault's 23rd FG at Kunming by the end of July. The pilots of 'Squadron X' had initially received tuition on the P-38 at the Fighter Training Centre near Casablanca.

Those who would travel to Kunming included future aces 1Lts Lee Gregg (a 1st FG veteran with one P-38 victory to his credit) and Bob Schultz (a man with some experience in photo-reconnaissance F-4s and F-5s), as well as 1Lt Tom Harmon (a B-25 pilot who was eager to fly the Lightning in combat). The flight would stage through Karachi, and include ten pilots accompanying the first P-38 fighters to reach China (on 25 July 1943).

Chennault was initially enthusiastic about receiving relatively modern fighting aircraft, even if they were older G-model Lightnings. The unsubstantiated but intriguing story, however, is that Chennault arranged a demonstration for interested dignitaries in which a P-38 was pitted in mock combat against one of his P-40s. Apparently, the Warhawk unit that provided the example used in the contest fixed

1Lt Bob Schultz poses beside his P-38G-10 42-13437 *Golden Eagle* circa 25 November 1943. Between August 1943 and March 1944 Schultz shot down five enemy aircraft (four in 1943), claimed a sixth as a probable and damaged a seventh while flying this aircraft (*Bates*)

the outcome by supplying a 'souped up', stripped down fighter flown by an expert on the type. Unsurprisingly, the outcome was less than flattering to the P-38, and it coloured Chennault's view of the Lockheed fighter from then.

He subsequently complained that the Lightning used too much precious fuel and that the P-40 was quite adequate for combat with Japanese types. Perhaps nobody suggested to him that the P-38 could travel twice as far, was faster and could climb to heights unreachable by the Warhawk. In any case, 'Squadron X' became the 449th FS on 2 August 1943, and it was ready for operations 24 days later. By then several successful missions had been flown by the unit whilst it was still known as 'Squadron X'.

Other pilots arrived to fill the squadron's ranks, and P-40 ace Maj Edmund Goss was appointed to lead the P-38 neophytes until Capt Sam Palmer took command in August. Under Goss' leadership, however, the squadron achieved three confirmed and two probable victories in late July. The unit also suffered its first loss on the very day it arrived at Kunming. 1Lt Enslen Lewden was initially the squadron's leading scorer, having claimed two confirmed victories and two probables by the end of July.

On 20 August Nakajima Ki-44 'Tojos' of the 85th Sentai and 'Oscars' of the 25th Sentai claimed to have shot down three P-40s by carefully avoiding the high altitude P-38s at Lingling. The next day the Lightning pilots exacted a modicum of revenge when 30 Japanese bombers, escorted by 25 'Oscars' of the 33rd Sentai, attacked Hengyang from high altitude. Nine P-38s led by Maj Goss dived on the enemy fighters at 30,000 ft and achieved one confirmed victory and three probably destroyed. Goss claimed one of the probables, while his wingman, 1Lt Robert Schultz, claimed another.

A dive-bombing attack on Canton on 10 September was covered by two P-38s of the 449th flown by 1Lts Lee Gregg and Wallace Weber. They dived in pursuit of what they took to be a pair of Japanese fighters attacking the dive-bombers, but when they closed on the enemy machines they counted no fewer than 16 JAAF fighters – 'Oscars' from the 25th Sentai and 'Tojos' from the 85th Sentai.

As the dive-bombers were withdrawing from the target Gregg and Weber exercised the better part of valour and turned away from the superior Japanese force. However, when they saw a lone Japanese single-engined fighter nearby they attacked. Their Japanese pilot was apparently no novice, and he quickly got in behind the P-38s. After a pitched battle in which Weber's Lightning was badly damaged, Gregg managed to shoot the enemy fighter down. Both P-38s returned to Lingling, but Weber's fighter lost its control cables just as it touched down, rolling along the runway like a clattering duck. Gregg was subsequently credited with shooting down a 'Zero-sen' (his opponent was of course a Ki-43) and Weber claimed a 'Tojo' probably destroyed. During this period Capt Yoshiaki Nakahara of the 85th Sentai was lost in his Ki-44 in the Canton area. Gregg's victory was his second (he had claimed an Italian fighter destroyed in May 1943 while serving with the 71st FS/1st FG), and the first of six that would make him the 449th's top-scoring ace.

Following the damage inflicted on Weber's Lightning by the lone enemy fighter, Lt Gen Chennault claimed that he warned the P-38 pilots about their careless attitude towards the low-speed manoeuvrability of Japanese fighters in China. He advised them to adopt the P-40 units' high-speed diving tactic, and to avoid turning combat at all costs.

However, the majority of the 449th's pilots had already been indoctrinated into the strong points of the P-38 when engaging German and Italian fighters with the 1st, 14th and 82nd FGs in 1942/43. Indeed, they were fully aware of the Lightning's ability to climb away from an enemy and outturn a pursuing fighter within a full circle or two – the latter manoeuvre proved to be far more difficult to achieve against Japanese types though. They were also aware that the P-38 had used successful attack and evasion tactics when engaging Japanese fighters in the Southwest Pacific. The diving and climbing speeds of the Lightning were known to be useful at most altitudes above about 10,000 ft, and nobody advised the 449th's pilots to try dogfighting with Japanese 'Oscars' and 'Tojos'.

By the beginning of October 1943 the Ki-44-equipped 85th Sentai was based in the Canton and Hankow areas. It is possible that the 449th encountered this unit during a dive-bombing mission flown on 30 October. The weather had cleared after a spell of storms and heavy cloud, and eight bomb-laden P-38s were sent off to Kiukang (or Jiujiang), in the Hankow area. The 'Tojo' was not only considerably faster than the Lightning both in level flight and in a climb, it was more robust than either the Zero-sen or the 'Oscar'. These advantages could explain the result of the engagement on the 30th that cost the 449th four P-38s destroyed. In return, a single Ki-43 (from the 25th Sentai) and an unknown number of Ki-44s were claimed as shot down.

A book written by the unit's Capt Tom Harmon describes the engagement, but this has been criticised as fanciful by some historians. Bob Schultz was the first to observe the enemy when he called out six Zero-sens (the formation was of course engaged by Ki-43s and Ki-44s, not IJNAF fighters) at 6000 ft off to the left. Harmon noticed that the fighter-bombers had released their ordnance and were heading home. He dropped his external tanks and banked to the left, observing six more Japanese fighters coming from above. It was a trap!

Harmon turned head-on into the six Japanese fighters, which scattered, presumably out of respect for the firepower contained in the nose of the P-38. The outnumbered Lightning pilot went after one that broke away alone. Firing his four machine guns from directly behind in a dive, he saw the Japanese fighter's canopy fly off and flames stream back from its engine. Using all of his guns in another burst, Harmon watched the target dive away on fire. By now the P-38 dive-bombers were out of sight, having withdrawn from the target area. Harmon climbed for altitude, whereupon he observed another lone Japanese fighter below him. A quick dive brought him up behind the unwary enemy fighter,

The second 449th FS P-38G-10 flown by American football star 1Lt Tom Harmon. He was flying this aircraft (42-13415) when he became embroiled in the great aerial battle over Kiukiang on 30 October 1943 that saw eight P-38s take on more than a dozen JAAF fighters. Harmon claimed to have destroyed two 'Oscars' before he was himself shot down and forced to trek for 32 days back to base. The aircraft's nickname was inspired by Harmon's wife, the film star Elyse Knox – the first *LITTLE BUTCH* had a been a B-25. The cartoon figure above the nickname is bedecked in a University of Michigan football jersey that bears Harmon's college team number

and it reportedly blew up after Harmon's bursts shot off large pieces of its wing and fuselage.

This sort of aggression had its perils, however, and bullets fired from another fighter that had slipped in behind him struck Harmon's cockpit. Apparently, some of the projectiles hitting his aircraft were cannon shells, as Harmon reported explosions that tore into the fuel primer, starting a fire between his legs that soon flamed out of control. He tried to beat it out with his gloved hands, but the situation soon became hopeless. Harmon released the canopy and let himself be hurled out into the relative safety of the cool Chinese air.

Fortunately for P-38 pilots in the CBI the twin-boom layout of their fighter meant that it was easily recognisable to Allied troops, thus reducing the chances of the former being downed by friendly fire. Here, Chinese troops are enjoying the chance to see a Lightning at close quarters at the 449th FS's Kunming base in late 1943

Deploying the canopy of his parachute moments later, Harmon then panicked that he had done this a little too early for he saw that he was surrounded by JAAF fighters, and still had hundreds of feet to descend. Slumped under his parachute, he played dead for long enough to encourage the enemy pilots to depart. When he did venture a glance around he was relieved to see what he took to be Bob Schultz's P-38 rushing out of the trap. Harmon was also able to confirm that Schultz had downed two 'Tojos'.

Although burned about the head and arms, Harmon realised that he was lucky to be alive when he finally emerged from the lake into which he had descended. After a 32-day trek, he made it back to Lingling, where he was able to confirm his own as well as Schultz's claims. Three other P-38s had been shot down, with at least one pilot killed. The Japanese claimed all eight P-38s, but even with the four reported lost by the 449th, it was a severe blow to Lightning operations in China. The anti-P-38 faction in the Fourteenth Air Force hailed it as proof of the type's unsuitability to the theatre.

The Lightning's CBI rehabilitation was partly accomplished by a daring operation in November 1943. AVG veterans and aces Lt Cols David 'Tex' Hill and George McMillan returned to the theatre to assume command of the 23rd FG and the 449th FS, respectively. Both pilots were highly respected and capable leaders who were to prove worthy commanders.

Aerial reconnaissance revealed that the Japanese presence on Taiwan was being swelled by aircraft massing on airfields such as Xinzhu, on the northwest coast. Photographs showed the presence of about 150 Japanese bombers and transports, which were mostly being used for training and re-supplying units in China. An attack on these airfields was initially viewed as too risky, as there were enough Zero-sens in Taiwan to see off any USAAF formation that targeted the island from China. However, in late 1943, the P-51A was introduced into service with the 23rd FG, giving Lt Col Chennault the ability to cover any bombing raid with long-range fighters, including P-38s of the 449th FS and Mustangs of the 76th FS. Whatever Chennault felt about the Lightning, he knew the type could cover the distance and protect the bombers adequately.

Morale in the 449th had been badly affected by the 30 October mission, with Lightning pilots being clearly aware of the fact that the Fourteenth Air Force headquarters lacked confidence in the aircraft. Justifiably perhaps, the 449th felt that it was not flying the favoured Allied fighter in the Chinese air war. That situation would change dramatically following the Thanksgiving Day raid on Xinzhu airfield. Eight P-51As and eight P-38Hs were to escort 14 B-25s to the target, which was reportedly overcrowded with bombers and transports. On the evening of 24 November the 449th pilots assigned to the mission were assembled for a briefing. Although they were told to take their 'Mae West' life vests with them, the aviators were not informed of their objective. They were, however, ordered to observe complete radio silence and fly very low over the sea so as to ensure surprise when they reached the target.

At 0830 hrs on the 25th a P-51 was withdrawn from the mission with mechanical problems, leaving 29 USAAF combat aircraft to depart China and fly a circuitous route to Taiwan. The fighters were led by the B-25s, which carried navigators and navigation equipment. When the force reached the enemy coast the P-38 pilots had been briefed to forge ahead and deal with any Japanese aircraft in the way. Having flown 400+ miles across the China Sea at minimum altitude, the 449th now had to climb to 1000 ft as they crossed the coast of Taiwan at noon. A Japanese transport aircraft appeared to the south and 'Tex' Hill ordered Capt Sam Palmer to deal with the threat. Palmer quickly downed what was probably a Kawasaki Ki-56 'Thalia' of the JAAF. He would also claim another during the mission, as well as a Zero-sen, to become a P-38 ace. It was, however, a temporary elevation, as later assessments reduced his total to four.

Meanwhile, 1Lt Bob Schultz found excitement over the airfield itself. Having managed to get in behind a transport in the landing pattern, he

1Lt Hampton Boggs of the 459th FS/ 80th FG poses in the cockpit of his P-38H-5 42-66994 at Chittagong. The single kill marking beneath the cockpit of the fighter indicates that this photograph was taken sometime after Boggs had claimed his first victory (a 'Hamp') over Insein on 1 December 1943. By the end of his tour Boggs had been credited with nine aerial and four straging victories, plus three more aircraft damaged in the air (Hancock)

sent the aircraft down in flames. Schultz then saw a single-engined aircraft coming straight at him. He fired at it until it passed over his canopy, spraying oil over his windscreen and shedding pieces of fuselage until it, too, crashed onto the airfield. Schultz was an outspoken critic of the Nazi regime to the point that he was convinced he had shot down two German aircraft, namely a Junkers Ju 52/3m transport and Junkers Ju 87 Stuka! The transport was possibly another Ki-56, while the single-engined aircraft was tentatively identified as a Kawasaki Ki-32 light bomber, Allied codename 'Mary'. Schultz remained so anti-German that after the war he changed his surname to Shoals.

Other P-38 pilots claimed to have shot down seven Japanese aircraft, with more destroyed on the ground. The P-51 pilots were also credited with two Zero-sen victories, as well as aircraft on the ground. While the fighters strafed, the B-25s raced over the airfield and added to the destruction by causing damage to aircraft and installations. A final tally of 46 Japanese aircraft destroyed was claimed, many of them credited to the 449th whose pilots felt an immediate rise in morale.

The Japanese reaction to the Taiwan surprise raid was vigorous, with several attacks being made on Lingling during the first weeks of December. The 449th's CO Lt Col George McMillan intercepted a reconnaissance 'Dinah' (claimed as a 'Nick') on the 10th, claiming it as his fifth aerial victory after he had scored 4.5 kills while flying P-40Cs with the AVG in 1941/42. McMillan made his second claim as a P-38 pilot two days later when Ki-48 'Lily' bombers, escorted by 'Oscars' and 'Tojos', attacked Hengyang for the last time at the end of a two-week offensive. Some 11 JAAF aircraft were reportedly destroyed for the loss of two P-40s. McMillan and 1Lt Lee Gregg each claimed to have shot down a 'Tojo' while the enemy fighters were among the eight P-38 pilots fending off the Japanese escorts.

Although the 449th FS would be credited with more victories in 1944/45, thus restoring the Lightning's reputation in China, Lt Gen Chennault did not approve the request made by 1st Air Commando Group (ACG) leader Col Phillip Cochran that P-38s be transferred to his group.

OPERATIONS IN BURMA

Until recently, the 459th FS was thought to be the only USAAF squadron formed and disbanded without ever serving in the country of its origin. When it was activated in India on 1 September 1943, there was a pressing need for a fighter unit to exploit the P-38's special attributes and counter enemy forces that had occupied Burma.

At that time Japanese air and ground units were able to prevent supplies being sent to China, as well as threaten India with invasion of its eastern borders. As a result, late in October, a number of P-38Hs became available

Like a number of pilots within the 459th FS, future ace 1Lt Walter Duke had briefly flown frontline sorties with the P-40-equipped 89th FS in India prior to transferring across to the newly formed Lightning unit on 30 November 1943. He would claim ten victories, two probables and five damaged between 11 March and 23 May 1944. Duke was killed in action on 6 June 1944 over Myitche, Burma

This P-38H-5 (42-67004) was the assigned aircraft of 1Lt Harry Sealy, its *Haleakala* nickname meaning 'House of the Sun' in Hawaiian – Haleakala is the dormant volcano that dominates the island of Maui. Indeed, the fighter was flown by him on 26 December 1943 when the 459th FS strafed Anisakan airfield. The unit claimed three 'Oscars' confirmed destroyed, one probably destroyed and two others damaged, all on the ground. Sealy, who ended the war with 4.5 aerial and six strafing kills, was credited with a Ki-43 probably destroyed

to the Tenth Air Force in Kurmitola. Personnel were acquired from the 80th FG as well as the 385th FS of the P-51A-equipped 311th FG. This meant that ground personnel posted to the 459th were familiar with the P-38's Allison V-1710 engine from their experience with the P-40 and P-51A.

The new squadron worked up to operational pitch with enthusiasm during November 1943, with some of its personnel moving to Madras, India, to erect and test new P-38s that were quickly flown to Kurmitola. Training flights were undertaken at a breathtaking pace, with records indicating that operations were tentatively started at the end of the month. The 459th's early missions saw it providing fighter escorts for B-25s, with future aces 1Lt Hampton Boggs and 2Lt Burdett Goodrich participating in these sorties.

The first and most frequent JAAF unit to engage the 459th was the veteran 64th Sentai, equipped with Ki-43s. While the 459th was on operations in Burma the 64th was based initially at Mingaladon and then at Meiktila. The noted Japanese aces Tateo Kato, Goichi Sumino and Yohei Hinoki claimed the bulk of their victories while serving with this unit, and all three pilots engaged the 459th. Ranged against such experienced opponents, the group suffered a tough initiation into combat over Burma. Indeed, before the 459th was able to draw blood, it had lost three of its number, probably to the elite 64th Sentai. Their first loss, on 21 November, was Flt Off Edmund Bovitt, and others would be posted missing before the unit could make its own claims.

A particularly ambitious operation was mounted on 27 November when B-24s attacked Rangoon. Four 459th P-38s, accompanied by P-51As of the 311th FG, escorted the bombers on this extreme-range flight. The formation entered a 'whirlwind' of a fight just as the aircraft reached the critical point of their fuel supply. At least one bomber was lost and four P-51s were shot down – one of the Mustangs shot down was flown by the CO of the 311th FG, Col H R Melton, who was taken prisoner. The 459th FS formation was also badly mauled, with two of the four fighters being shot down. They probably fell victim to 64th Sentai ace Lt Yohei Hinoki, who claimed two P-38s destroyed that same day.

Yet, bitter as these losses were, the 459th quickly absorbed the lessons of combat and claimed its first victories in the same area on 1 December.

1Lt Hampton Boggs was flying P-38G-10 42-12994 over Insein, near Rangoon, when he claimed to have downed a 'Hamp' – his quarry was almost certainly a Ki-43. Another pilot claimed a Ki-45 'Nick', and a second twin-engined Japanese fighter was reported to have been probably destroyed.

Throughout 1944 the 459th would operate within the auspices of the Royal Air Force's No 224 Group alongside the USAAF's 1st ACG and the 311th FG, and claim more than 80 Japanese aircraft destroyed in the air and on the ground.

Northern Burma came under Allied control after the fall of Myitkyina in August 1944, by which time the 459th could claim to have played a major role in reducing the effect of Japanese air power in the area.

A foretaste of what lay in store for the squadron came on 26 December 1943 when it strafed the airfield at Anisakan in mission No 23. Several flights of P-38s, flying at treetop height over the forest, surprised the enemy at about 0810 hrs. 1Lt Walter Duke, flying the same aircraft that Hampton Boggs had used to claim a victory at the beginning of the month, was credited with destroying an 'Oscar' on the runway. Duke would subsequently become the squadron's leading ace with ten victories, prior to being posted missing in action on 6 June 1944.

Two other future aces also made their first claims on 26 December, Capt Maxwell Glenn (in P-38G-10 42-12998) damaging an 'Oscar' and 2Lt Burdett Goodrich being credited with another 'Oscar' probably destroyed. 1Lt Harry 'Lighthorse' Sealy, who ended the war with 4.5 aerial and six strafing kills, also claimed a Ki-43 as a probable. The total bag for this surprise mission was three 'Oscars' confirmed destroyed, one probably destroyed and two others damaged, all on the ground. It was perhaps an ominous portent for the JAAF in Burma.

Although the P-38 was distributed in small numbers in the CBI theatre, the fighter was able to establish an impressive record. Indeed, although outnumbered by P-40s and P-51s, the P-38 was flown by around 20 per cent of the theatre's aces.

Capt Max Glenn of the 459th FS is sitting in the cockpit of P-38H-5 *Sluggo-III* in late 1943, the future 7.5-victory ace subsequently claiming his first three kills in this aircraft in March and April 1944

MEDITERRANEAN ACTION

I n early November 1942 the remarkable range of the P-38 once again proved its worth when pilots from the 1st and 14th FGs were able to fly their fighters from England's south coast over the Bay of Biscay to Morocco in the wake of the Operation *Torch* landings. Enough of the twin-boomed fighters were available in Tafaroui, Algeria, for operations to commence by the 11th of the month.

The first real scoring opportunity for the aircraft in North Africa came on 22 November when 1Lt Mark Shipman of the 48th FS/14th FG accounted for an unidentified twin-engined Italian aircraft. Although he ultimately failed to 'make ace', Shipman would see plenty of action while flying P-38s both in North Africa and England, from where he undertook bomber escort missions. He subsequently claimed a six-engined Messerschmitt Me 323 Gigant transport and a Bf 109 shot down by the end of 1943.

The 14th FG's first opportunity for multiple kills came on 28 November when the group intercepted large formations of Italian transports and German bombers. P-38 pilots claimed to have shot down eight Savoia-Marchetti SM.81 Pipistrello transports, five Ju 52/3m transports and a Ju 88 bomber for no loss. 1Lt Virgil Smith of the 48th FS claimed the Ju 88 as the first of his eventual six victories, while his squadronmate, 1Lt Ervin Ethell, reported downing four Ju 52/3ms, with a Bf 109 as a probable. With this haul he almost became the premier P-38 ace.

Part of the new Twelfth Air Force in North Africa, the five squadrons of the 1st and 14th FGs were introduced to the grim realities of war in this theatre when they were required to provide cover for advancing troops with strafing and dive-bombing attacks, rather than provide fighter escort for bombers. Seasoned Luftwaffe pilots exploited these ground attack missions because they made the P-38s vulnerable to interception from above. By the end of 1942, therefore, the Lightning units were sustaining severe losses, even though they had proved their value as the best USAAF fighter in theatre. Due to the high attrition rate suffered by the Twelfth Air Force, there was soon a shortage of both P-38s and P-40s in North Africa. In the case of the Lockheed fighter the need was so great that every serviceable example that could be found in the UK was quickly despatched to Algeria.

Limited numbers was not the only disadvantage facing the P-38 units. Although there were enough fighters to supply five squadrons – the 27th, 71st and 94th FSs of the 1st FG and 48th and 49th FSs of the 14th FG – in November 1942, the battle-hardened German and Italian pilots soon had the measure of their inexperienced American opponents, hence the high attrition rate. To make matters worse, the tactics initially employed by the USAAF were not the most effective.

German pilots were particularly adept at climbing above escorted American bombers to find the most advantageous position from which

Premier P-38 ace 1Lt Virgil Smith of the 48th FS/14th FG poses in front of his P-38F-1 *"KNIPTION"* (serial unknown) in England during the autumn of 1942. Within weeks of this photograph being taken, Smith and the rest of the 14th FG were embroiled in the battle for North Africa. Achieving ace status on 12 December 1942, Smith claimed a sixth victory 48 hours prior to being killed in action on 30 December

to attack. The bombers' escorts were obliged to watch the dust rising from enemy airfields as German and Italian interceptors were free to climb to superior heights.

Aside from the policy of sticking close to the bombers, P-38 pilots in North Africa employed tactics that delighted Luftwaffe fighter pilots, who considered them not only ineffective but also dangerous to the American pilots themselves. Weaving in great arcs at very low or very high altitudes, the P-38s were relatively easy to attack and defeat. Only after painful losses were incurred did the USAAF units learn to fight efficiently and, eventually, become quite deadly in their engagements with Axis aircraft.

Nevertheless, even with the poor combat tactics in use at the end of 1942, the eager P-38 pilots were able to shoot down Axis transport aircraft, bombers and even fighters in engagements that offered mixed success. The first Luftwaffe victories over the P-38 were recorded by *Jagdgeschwader* (JG) 53, which claimed to have downed seven of the Lockheed fighters on 28 November.

The 1st FG had quite a scrap with a formation of Bf 110 *Zerstörers* the next day when several burgeoning P-38 aces opened or added to their scores. Amongst the former were 1Lt Jack Ilfrey and Capt Newell Roberts of the 94th FS, who each shared in the destruction of a Bf 110 while returning from a mission to Gabes airfield. From January 1943 the awarding of partial or shared victories was discontinued by the Twelfth Air Force, although this confused rather than cleared up the contemporary claims situation. Initially, at least one of the Bf 110 claims made by Ilfrey and Roberts was shared with the 14th FG, but examination of the combat reports indicates that both Ilfrey and Roberts should be awarded a whole victory each.

The outcome of a combat on 2 December was a good deal clearer, and it resulted in the same pilots from the 1st FG adding to their scores. Capt Roberts was the leader of the P-38 flight that engaged the Bf 109s over Gabes airfield, and his combat report offers a succinct account of the part he played in the mission;

'I took off at 0645 hrs on a fighter sweep of Faid, which we were to strafe so that American ground forces could move in. Lts McWherter, Ilfrey and Lovell were in the flight with me. We shot up three gun posts at Faid from 0720 hrs to 0725 hrs and then headed for Sfax. We flew along the coast at between 0 ft to 500 ft, and when we reached Gabes we came down the west side of the airfield and saw four Me 109s taking off. I hit the third one, giving it a long burst that caused it to blow up in the air. I hit another Me 109 at about 200 ft and saw thick black smoke pouring from it. Lt McWherter saw this plane crash to the ground.'

Jack Ilfrey also claimed two Bf 109s, the future ace having had to perform some wild evasive manoeuvres that saw his fighter take several heavy hits. Uffz Forster of 5./JG 53 claimed to have shot a P-38 down at an altitude of about 150 m (480 ft) some 40 km (25 miles) west of Gabes at around the time of this action, so it is possible that he thought he had downed Ilfrey.

First Lightning Ace

The only thing certain about the first P-38 ace is that he was created sometime between 12 and 26 December 1942. Jack Ilfrey and Virgil Smith were accomplished P-38 pilots from the 1st and 14th FGs, and both

Capt Newell Roberts of the 94th FS/ 1st FG was one of the first aces of the North African campaign, having scored five victories by 9 February 1943

Seven-victory ace 2Lt Ward Kuentzel of the 96th FS/82nd FG discusses the operation of his P-38's four 0.50-in machine guns with his armourer, Cpl Howard Shaffner. Kuentzel was posted missing in action on 19 June 1944 while serving with the 434th FS/479th FG in the ETO

Capt Joel Owens pictured with his 27th FS P-38F. By the end of the North African campaign, Owens had scored three victories while serving as CO of the 27th FS of the 1st FG and two more with the 14th FG after he became the group's deputy CO (*Cook*)

achieved success during the difficult period of early combat in North Africa. Under the Twelfth Air Force's initial system of shared victory scoring, Ilfrey was credited with 4.5 victories by 26 December and Smith had 3.85 kills, with a half-share in a Bf 109 and a third-share in a Ju 52/3m. With the change of policy Ilfrey and Smith both had five victories. Then, on 28 December, Smith added a sixth when he was credited with shooting down a Bf 109. Forty-eight hours later he was killed while attempting a crash-landing in a battle-damaged P-38 near Gabes. He may have been the 35th victim of 85-kill ace Ofw Herbert Rollwage of 5./JG 53, who claimed his first P-38 victory 30 km (19 miles) northwest of Gabes at the approximate time Smith was lost.

December also saw the arrival of the P-38-equipped 82nd FG in North Africa – a unit that was to produce the Twelfth Air Force's top-scoring ace. 2Lt William 'Dixie' Sloan had not only gained 12 victories by the end of July 1943, his first success was also the 82nd FG's premier confirmed claim. Sloan was something of a maverick who went after enemy aircraft while the rest of the group adhered to strict discipline. The 82nd was remarkable in having its victories distributed among many different pilots, while a few of the highest-scoring aces like Sloan and Frank Hurlbut displayed a high degree of personal initiative. For his first kill, on 7 January 1943, Sloan revealed a penchant for closing with the enemy when he shot down one of six Bf 109s that he encountered during a mission escorting B-26s to Gabes. He later attempted to explain away his success by claiming he was extremely frightened, and that the enemy fighter was blocking his route back to base!

Another 96th FS pilot who was on the same mission and also admitted to being scared was future ace 2Lt Claude Kinsey. He had been a sergeant pilot with Sloan back in the United States before all USAAF aviators had to be commissioned for deployment overseas. He reported;

'Frankly, I was frightened. Looking back, I could see a ship with the whole leading edge of his wing blinking flame at me. It was not a very nice thing to look at and, I'm telling you, I didn't look at it for long! Everything went forward in the cockpit and I was indicating well over 400 mph. I lost him and zoomed up and over and back to where the fight was. I picked out a ship but I couldn't get my sight on him for long enough to do any good. I made another pass at him and then rejoined the bombers. I was escorting them and had to stick to them.'

The following day 2Lt Thomas 'Ace' White of the 97th FS claimed the first of his six victories when he shot down an Fw 190 while escorting B-26s attacking Kairouan airfield. This was the 82nd FG's second confirmed claim and the first for the 97th FS. White reported;

'While acting as part of an escort for B-26s my airplane [P-38F number 42-12614] was attacked from the left side by a Focke Wulf 190. I made a steep climbing turn to the left, which enabled me to fire a long burst into the entire left side of the enemy aircraft. Tracer bullets were seen to enter his entire ship. His ship started smoking badly, shudder and then went into a violent spin and crashed. Verification of this report is made by 1Lt Albert R Hahn, S-2 Officer of the 17th Bombardment Group, whose interrogation of three bomber crews that were being escorted stated that the enemy aircraft crashed to the ground.'

Other German fighters were claimed during a 1st FG mission that same day, which saw the group escorting B-17s to Ferryville. But the 8th proved to be a day of disaster for eight P-38 pilots of the 14th FG who were strafing tanks during a low-level sweep over Kairouan. JG 2 ace Kurt Bühligen claimed to have shot down a 49th FS P-38, which was one of at least six credited to his formation of approximately 20 Luftwaffe fighters. The incident left him with a low opinion of the Lockheed fighter, three of which were immediately lost. One exploded in mid air, another was seen burning on the ground and a third was abandoned by its pilot after he managed to down one of the Bf 109s and then zoom up to 500 ft before bailing out. A fourth Lightning that was badly shot up limped back to the airfield at Youks-les-Bains, where it crash-landed.

Four out of eight P-38s lost, with crews either killed or wounded, was typical of the arithmetic of missions flown by the hard-pressed crews over the desert in 1942/43. Eight Lightning squadrons with too few aircraft and pilots in need of relief proved to be too much of a strain for the Twelfth Air Force. The break finally came at the end of January 1943 when the two available 14th FG squadrons simply had too few aircraft and crews to continue operations – the group had lost six P-38s in combat on 23 January alone. XII Fighter Command was compelled to withdraw the remaining crews, leaving only the undermanned 1st and 82nd FGs to continue the fight for the final three months of the North African campaign. The 14th FG would re-enter the Mediterranean war in May 1943, rearmed and ready to write the rest of its impressive record.

CAMPAIGN EVALUATION

Kurt Bühligen might have dismissed the P-38 during the early Mediterranean operations, but Ofw Herbert Kaiser, an 8./JG 77 ace who scored his first Lightning kill (his 57th victory in a total of 68) on 8 January 1943, considered the P-38 to be generally faster and more manoeuvrable than his unit's Bf-109G-6s. The underwing cannon gondolas made the G-6 more cumbersome and compromised maximum speed and turning performance. Kaiser stated that he used no special tactics in combat when engaging the P-38, but simply regarded it with a great deal of respect.

Fellow high-scoring ace Ofw Johann Pichler of 7./JG 77 accounted for at least three P-38s, including one on 24 June 1943 for his 35th confirmed claim. He was most appreciative of the Lightning's qualities as an opponent. The first time Pichler encountered the type over North Africa his flight was able to slip behind an unwary group of four P-38s and open fire. He was dumbstruck by the alerted enemy's ability to climb swiftly away and accelerate rapidly, leaving the Messerschmitts far behind.

Although the P-38 was criticised for its poor initial roll rate, this was offset somewhat by its impressive acceleration – a feature that saved many pilots from immediate disaster. Legendary 176-victory ace Maj Johannes Steinhoff, who was *Geschwaderkommodore* of JG 77 during 1943, claimed three P-38s whilst defending airfields around Foggia, in Italy, from attack on 25 August 1943. All available Lightnings in the Mediterranean theatre had flown at wave-top height across the sea to attack the airfields, where they reportedly destroyed at least 35 aircraft

1Lt Bill Schildt of the 95th FS/ 82nd FG was photographed with his last Lightning (P-38G-15 43-2406) at around the time he completed his combat tour on 17 July 1943. He had claimed six victories between 29 January and 14 May 1943

Capt Ernie 'Hawk' Osher of the 95th FS/82nd FG poses with his famous mount P-38F-15 43-2112 *THE "SAD SACK"* and its groundcrew at Berteaux, Algeria, after scoring his fifth victory with the fighter on 11 May. These men are, from left to right, TSgt Leroy Lee (crew chief), Sgt Bill Coy (assistant crew chief), Cpl Sorvando Velarde (armourer) and Capt Osher. When this photograph was taken *THE "SAD SACK"* had flown 'only' 86 of its eventual total of 183 combat missions. This P-38 was considered to have been one of the few fighters that had been perfectly constructed. Pilots flying 43-2112 had reputedly claimed 16 victories by the time the Lightning was taken out of service in mid-1944

1Lt 'Ricky' Zubarik of the 96th FS/ 82nd FG sits on the windscreen of his *Pearl III* (P-38G-10 42-13054), camera in hand, right after becoming an ace on 13 May 1943 – as indicated by the five swastikas on the fuselage of the fighter. He scored his final victory on the 21st, three days before he was shot down over Sardinia and made a PoW. The question marks are for the two Me 410s (claimed as 'Me 210s') that collided while chasing him and *Pearl III* on 6 May, for which he received no official credit

on the ground and shot down several others.

Like his pilots, Steinhoff respected the P-38's ability to turn almost within its own length and change from being the hunted to the hunter. He also shared in their appreciation of the type's ability to 'zoom climb'. Finally, the Lightning's armament was also feared by Axis aircrew.

In the period between the withdrawal of the 14th FG at the end of January 1943 and its return to operations after the campaign ended in North Africa in May, there were a number of successful actions where pilots relied heavily on the P-38's fighting qualities. There were also some severe losses. The 82nd FG in particular enjoyed some early successes, and by the end of January its pilots had accounted for 13 German aircraft destroyed without loss. In fact, Luftwaffe pilots claimed to have shot down only three P-38s in North Africa during that period, including one for Oblt Bühligen on 28 January.

2Lt 'Dixie' Sloan claimed his second kill – a Bf 109 that he reported shooting down north of Gabes – on the 30th, and he would add his fifth (a Bf 109) on 15 February after claiming another Bf 109 and a rare Do 217 bomber 13 days earlier. Future aces Capt Ernest Osher and 2Lt Bill Schildt of the 95th FS achieved their first kills on 29 January over El Aouina airfield. Schildt would claim a Bf 110 two days later over the Gulf of Tunis to score his second confirmed kill.

The 96th FS's 2Lt Claude Kinsey also reported shooting down a Bf 109 on 29 January, and he doubled his tally the following day with another Messerschmitt destroyed north of Gabes. Having downed three Italian aircraft in February and March to 'make ace', Kinsey claimed his sixth and

seventh victories on 5 April over the Mediterranean Sea off Cap Bon during Operation *Flax* – a campaign by Allied fighters to intercept Axis transport aircraft attempting to fly supplies to German and Italian units in Tunisia. More than 100 Axis aircraft, including Ju 52/3ms, Bf 109s, Bf 110s, Ju 87s and Ju 88s, as well as several Italian types, were claimed by the P-38 pilots of the 1st and 82nd FGs between 5 and 11 April. The venerable Ju 52/3m bore the brunt of these losses, with 70+ examples of the Junkers tri-motor being shot down. The success of *Flax* virtually wiped out logistical support for Axis forces retreating towards the Tunisian coast.

But Kinsey was badly wounded either by return fire from one of the Ju 87s he had shot down or by 'friendly' fire from one of his own comrades in a P-38. With his Lightning ablaze, he climbed from 50 ft to 400 ft as he struggled to release his seat belt. Kinsey finally bailed out and landed in the water. Struggling ashore, he found that his wounds were so severe that he was unable to move. Local people found him and turned him over to the Italians, who provided minimal treatment until he was passed on to the Germans following Italy's capitulation in September 1943.

While Kinsey was waiting to be transported to Germany, and captivity, he and another 96th FS ace, 1Lt Charles 'Shorty' Zubarik, plotted to escape. Kinsey made it through the wire but Zubarik was stopped when he hesitated, and consequently spent the rest of the conflict as a prisoner of war (PoW). Despite many difficulties, including an arduous trek around the Apennines, Kinsey reached advancing Canadian troops on 22 October and was sent home to recover. On his way back Kinsey managed to stop at the 82nd's new base at Lecce to discover that he had been promoted to first lieutenant shortly after he had been shot down.

Several P-38 aces emerged during Operation *Flax*, including 1Lt Lee Wiseman of the 1st FG's 71st FS. Having downed an Fw 190 on 4 February, he claimed two Ju 52/3ms and a Macchi C.200 on 10 April and a second Fw 190 two days later. Squadronmate 1Lt Meldrum Sears, who already had two victories to his name, accounted for four Ju 52/3ms on the 10th, with a Bf 109 downed on the 12th. After the war that final kill was confirmed to put him level with Claude Kinsey as the North African campaign's top P-38 ace.

2Lt Ray Crawford of the 82nd FG's 97th FS shot down two Ju 52/3ms on 10 April to 'make ace', and he was credited with a sixth victory in mid June. 2Lt John Mackay of the 1st FG's 27th FS claimed to have downed two Ju 52/3ms and a rare Fw 189 twin-boom reconnaissance aircraft on 5 April, taking his tally to four kills. He would achieve two more aerial victories on 25 May in an interesting engagement. The 27th FS had just attacked an Axis airfield on the island of Sicily when it was bounced by a formation of more than 20 Bf 109s and Fw 190s of JG 53 north of San Vito lo Capo. In the 25-minute battle that ensued, the unit claimed to have accounted for 11 German fighters for the loss of three P-38s. Mackay was credited with two Bf 109s for his fifth and sixth victories. Coincidentally, 8 and 9 *Staffeln* of JG 53 claimed three P-38s northwest of Trapani, Sicily, on 25 May.

INVASION OF ITALY

With the final surrender of Axis forces in North Africa, the Allies turned their attention to the Italian mainland, as well as their islands in the

Maj Darrell Welch claimed to have shot down two Bf 109s over Tripoli and Bizerte between January and March 1943 while serving with the 27th FS/1st FG. He also claimed three Ju 52/3ms during the April 1943 interdiction of Axis air supply routes to Tunisia. Bearing kill markings for all five of Welch's victories, the P-38F-1 parked behind him in this photograph was almost certainly the fighter that he had flown from England in early November 1942 when the 1st FG had been ordered to participate in the *Torch* landings in North Africa (*Cook*)

2Lt Larry Liebers (left) of the 96th FS/ 82nd FG chats with his crew chief, TSgt Roswell Harding, on the wing of his P-38 whilst assistant crew chief Sgt Leroy Garman and armourer Cpl Wendell Stoltz work on the fighter's weaponry. 2Lt Liebers shot down an Fw 190 near Benevento, in Italy, on 20 August 1943 for his seventh, and last, victory. He completed his tour at the end of that month

Mediterranean. The campaign against the latter escalated in June, with the P-38 units escorting Allied medium and heavy bombers targeting Axis airfields. These missions were vigorously opposed by Axis fighters, and the 96th FS in particular enjoyed significant success on 18 June when its pilots accounted for 13 Axis fighters, including more than ten Italian aircraft, over the Gulf of Aranci. Amongst the pilots to make claims was Flt Off Frank Hurlbut, who shot down his third and fourth enemy aircraft when he claimed a Bf 109 and a Reggiane Re.2001 destroyed. Squadronmate 2Lt Larry Liebers claimed to have downed more Italian aircraft (five in total) than any other P-38 pilot after he shot down two C.202s and a C.205 just before 1000 hrs over the Gulf.

Italian fighter pilots shared the German view that the P-38 was a devil of an opponent, even though it sometimes appeared to be easy to shoot down. Perhaps they too had seen Lightnings apparently bursting into flames, heralding their demise, when of course such a display simply meant the pilot had opened the throttles. As previously noted, when the throttles were suddenly advanced in an effort to evade an attacking enemy, there was a great deal of smoke and a flash of flame emitted from the engine waste gates. This display of apparently heavy damage perhaps made the P-38 look mortally wounded, convincing some enemy pilots on its tail that it was plummeting to its doom. The P-47 also had this tendency, which wrapped the tail of the Republic fighter in smoke and flame, perhaps giving the premature impression of the aircraft's demise.

For their part, P-38 pilots who met Italian fighters in combat thought that they were not particularly dangerous, despite their impressive manoeuvrability.

2Lt Paul Wilkins and his groundcrew pose for the camera atop their P-38G in late 1943. If this fighter is the 37th FS's aircraft number '86' then it may well be the Lightning flown by Maj Bill Leverette during his record-setting mission of 9 October 1943. Wilkins, who claimed three kills in 1943, 'made ace' in January 1944 (Blake)

There was more success for the 82nd FG's growing band of aces during the early phase of the Operation *Husky* landings on Sicily. Supporting the amphibious assault on Gela on 10 July, the 96th FS accounted for ten Axis aircraft, including, a C.200, a Ju 88 and an Fw 190, which took 1Lt 'Dixie' Sloan's score to 11. A Bf 109 represented 1Lt Ed Waters' seventh, and last, victory, while 2Lt Larry Liebers' Fw 190 was his sixth success. Three more Focke-Wulf fighter-bombers downed by Flt Off Frank Hurlbut made him an ace.

Schlachtgeschwader 10 was one of the Axis units engaged by the 96th on the 10th, its Fw 190 fighter-bombers suffering heavy losses after they were set upon by the P-38s. The CO of I./SG 10, Maj Egon Thiem, was forced to abandon his Fw 190 near the town of Corleone after its engine was set on fire. He had been attacked by fighters from the 96th FS while his unit was attempting to bomb Allied troop transport vessels. The P-38 pilots chased Thiem northwards through valleys and mountains, finally getting him in their gunsights and forcing him to zoom high enough to bail out from his Fw 190. Thiem was almost certainly shot down by an ace.

P-38 pilots had another good day on 18 July when the 14th FG accounted for 15 Ju 52/3ms off Ischia. 2Lt Lloyd Hendrix scored his only victories of the war when he claimed four of the transports, while 2Lt Paul Wilkins of the 37th FS made the first of his five victory claims (the last two came in January 1944) when he downed two more. Capt Herbert Ross of the 48th FS also got a pair of tri-motors for his second and third victories – his tally would stand at seven kills by the time he finished his tour in October. Finally, squadronmate 1Lt Sidney Weatherford accounted for two more as his third and fourth of five confirmed victories.

In return, Luftwaffe fighter pilots claimed to have shot down two P-38s during the course of the day, presumably in the same general area. Ltn Otto Wessling of 10./JG 3 claimed his 70th victory when he downed a P-38, while 8./ZG 26 Bf 110 pilot Uffz Wilhelm Reiner was also credited with a Lightning shot down.

One of the most celebrated P-38 missions of 1943 was the surprise raid on the cluster of Axis airfields on the Foggia plain on 25 August. Lt Col George MacNicol, CO of the 82nd FG, led the fighter force at wave-top height, with a navigator's compass between his feet, to ensure surprise. This was achieved when the P-38s appeared over the airfields and duly destroyed 34 enemy aircraft and damaged many more. Heavy bombers completed the job during the second phase of the attack, leaving more than 100 aircraft destroyed or damaged. Five P-38s were reported missing in action, this figure presumably including the three claimed by the CO of JG 77, Maj Johannes Steinhoff.

Two days later one of the ranking aces of the crack 82nd FG

Sidney Weatherford (seen here with the rank of major later in the war) of the 48th FS accounted for two of the Ju 52/3ms claimed by the 14th FG on 18 July 1943. The downed tri-motor transports took Weatherford's score to four, and he 'made ace' with a Bf 109 destroyed on 26 August 1943 (*Sidney Weatherford*)

This publicity photograph of six 82nd FG aces was taken in mid-July 1943. They are, from left to right, 2Lt Ward Kuentzel (96th FS), Flt Off Frank Hurlbut (96th) and 2Lts Ray Crawford (97th), Larry Liebers (96th), 'Dixie' Sloan (96th) and Lou Curdes (95th)

1Lt Leslie 'Andy' Andersen (on the right), who joined the 96th FS in June 1943, scored his first two kills and a probable (all Bf 109s) during the 82nd FG's 2 September DUC mission. In this photograph he is posing with his squadronmates 1Lt Dana Lovejoy (on the left) and Capt Bradley Prann at Lecce, in Italy, in November 1943. Andersen downed two more Bf 109s on 6 December and another Messerschmitt four days later to achieve ace status. Unfortunately, no photograph could be located of Andersen's assigned aircraft, P-38G-10 42-13026 *Pugnacious Peggy*, which was later transferred to the Fifteenth Air Force's 154th Weather Reconnaissance Squadron (*Fred Selle*)

completed his remarkable scoring run in the Mediterranean when he became an unwilling guest of the Germans. 2Lt Louis Curdes was one of the most aggressive pilots in the 95th FS, having claimed the destruction of three Bf 109s, with another damaged, over Cap Bon on 29 April 1943. He followed this up with two more Messerschmitts on 19 May over the Sardinian town of Villacidro. Curdes' sixth claim was for a C.202 downed over the Gulf of Aranci on 24 June.

The 95th FS had become involved in a major battle over Benevento, in southwest Italy, on 27 August. Curdes had claimed two Bf 109s destroyed before he in turn was forced to crash-land his damaged P-38 on a beach. He then simply got out of the wreckage of his aircraft and waited dejectedly for capture. Curdes soon found that being a PoW did not suit him, so he took the first opportunity to escape and returned to Allied-held territory in May 1944!

He then requested a return to combat duty, and was back in action with the 4th Air Command Squadron (ACS) of the 3rd ACG in the Pacific later in the year. The side of Curdes' Mustang was adorned with a variety of victory markings – German, Italian and Japanese (he downed a 'Dinah' while flying a P-51D with the 4th ACS on 7 February 1945). There was also a single American flag, which recalled the C-47 that he had crippled in an attempt to stop it landing in error on a Japanese-held airstrip on Batan Island, in the Philippines. Curdes returned to flying P-38s when he transferred to the 49th FG near the end of the war.

Two missions that were to prove costly to P-38 units of the Twelfth Air Force were flown on 30 August and 2 September 1943. The Luftwaffe's JGs 3, 53 and 77 were now on the defensive in the Naples area, and on the 30th they managed to intercept Allied bomber formations being escorted by P-38s. Although the German aircraft did minimal damage to the bombers, they achieved significant results against the P-38s of the 1st FG. Escorting B-26s targeting the marshalling yards at Aversa, the USAAF aircraft ran into a mixed formation of Axis fighters. The 1st was awarded a Distinguished Unit Citation (DUC) for its part in the mission (it had also received one following the Foggia raid five days earlier), the combat account that accompanied the decoration graphically describing the action;

'Crossing the Italian coast, their formation of 44 P-38s was intercepted by approximately 75 aggressive and highly persistent enemy aircraft. Alone and unaided, the 1st FG engaged them, beating off wave after wave of enemy planes attempting to pierce the fighter defences and break up the bomber formation. These courageous pilots fought a brilliant defensive aerial battle, destroying eight, probably destroying three and damaging three enemy fighters, while our own losses totalled 13 missing. Through their highly effective cover, the bomber formation was able to complete a highly successful bombing run unmolested, and return to base without the loss of a single bomber.'

This was the most costly in a series of bloody missions for the 1st FG in particular, and all P-38 units in the Mediterranean theatre in general.

Two of the 13 downed pilots, did however, evade capture and return to the group.

On 2 September the 82nd FG would earn its second DUC in 11 days during a remarkably similar mission to the same area. The group fielded a maximum effort force of 74 P-38s to protect 72 B-25s of the 321st Bombardment Group that were targeting Naples' Cancello marshalling yards. Before the day was over the 82nd would engage the same enemy units faced by the 1st FG on 30 August, and lose ten of its number in the process.

Ten days short of his 21st birthday, Flt Off Frank Hurlbut of the 96th FS/82nd FG returned from the 10 July 1943 mission tired but happy, having scored three confirmed victories (all Fw 190s) southwest of Sicily to become an ace

It was not until the bombers turned away from the target that the Axis fighters struck. As the B-25s pointed their noses downward to pick up speed for the withdrawal, 15 to 20 enemy fighters dived on them. Both Bf 109s and C.202s were identified in the group that tore into the 96th FS to initiate an old-fashioned turning dogfight. The Lightning pilots turned into the attack, but they soon became so embroiled in the combat that cries for assistance were heard from the embattled aviators. Below them, the bombers were on their way out of the target area, allowing the P-38 pilots to concentrate their efforts on the additional German and Italian fighters that were now joining the battle.

Pilots from the 95th FS had already claimed several enemy fighters when they noticed that the bombers were now well clear of the action down at an altitude of about 4000 ft. It was now their turn to try to extricate themselves from the battle that was driving them ever lower towards the coast. This task then became even harder when around 30 more Axis fighters pitched into the fray with the 96th FS. The unit's 2Lt Fred Selle claimed three Bf 109s shot down (his only claims), but also saw 2Lt James Padgett collide with another Messerschmitt just off his wing. Although Padgett was able to take to his parachute, the German pilot apparently perished when he failed to extricate himself from the remains of his fighter before it crashed.

The 96th claimed 11 of the group's 23 victories that day, but it paid a high price for this success – seven of the ten P-38s lost by the 82nd FG came from this unit. Amongst the pilots credited with kills was 2Lt Leslie Andersen, who achieved the first two of his eventual five aerial victories when he claimed two Bf 109s north of Ischia. The author interviewed Andersen some years ago, and put to him the proposition that the P-38 could pull a very tight turn if indicated airspeed was reduced to about 140 mph. Andersen's jaw almost visibly dropped as he replied, 'Why would anybody in his right mind want to lose that much airspeed? Just keep turning, and the '38 will lose its opponent'.

Flt Off Frank Hurlbut got the last of his nine victories over Axis airmen during this combat when he claimed a Bf 109 north of Ischia. He subsequently recalled;

'We had fought our way down to the water so they couldn't hit us from below – only from the sides or from above. This gave us a little less to

Pilots who participated in the classic Stuka interception mission of 9 October 1943 are identified here as, from left to right, Thomas Smith, Homer Sprinkle, Harry Troy Hanna, Wayne Blue, Bill Leverette, Robert Margison and Wilmer La Rue. This photograph was probably taken just after the mission, and aircraft number '86', usually flown by 2Lt Paul Wilkins, was the P-38 Leverette used on the mission (*Blake*)

worry about. Two Me 109s in line astern dove down right next to me, then pulled up and away to the right. I broke into them as they came down, only to find that I had been suckered away from my flight, which had continued to the left, just above the water. Immediately thereafter, two other '109s attacked me from above. They were flying line abreast and came in to close range. I could see their guns flashing as I looked back and up through my canopy. At the same time, two more Me 109s, flying close together, were closing in from approximately 90 degrees directly above my canopy, firing as they came.

'I was in a maximum performance turn to the left and an extreme cross-controlled skid to the right. This was a trick I had learned that I used in combat many times. When enemy fighters were trying to hit me I would bank violently whilst cross-controlling, standing on the inside rudder and racking the aircraft into a turn. This caused the aeroplane to slide sideways and fly erratically in a somewhat different flight path from the direction it *appeared* to be going in. This technique probably saved my life once again, because even though all four enemy aircraft were right on top of me, and the water just below was churning from cannon and machine gun fire, they all completely missed me – thank God!

'As I was getting back with the other P-38s in the area, another single Me 109 was down at my level. The pilot was banking around to the right and cutting directly in front of me. I straightened out my aircraft for a few seconds, led him with my guns and started firing. He flew right through my line of fire and then simply peeled over and went into the sea. I wasn't sure whether he had gone in because of my fire or had simply forgotten in the heat of battle what his altitude was when he peeled away.'

German records indicate that at least seven Bf 109s were lost, with five pilots missing. There is no mention of the single Fw 190 that was claimed to have been destroyed. Italian records regarding the four Macchi fighters reported as downed are not available. The missing German pilots included Ltn Franz Schiess, the *Staffelführer* of 8./JG 53 with 67 victories to his credit – 17 of these were P-38s, seven of which he had claimed in the previous 13 days. Only two of the ten 82nd FG pilots shot down in the battle survived to become PoWs. JGs 3, 53 and 77 – the German units that had engaged the 82nd FG that day and the 1st FG on 30 August – comprised many of the best Luftwaffe pilots in the Mediterranean theatre. Men such as Oblt Gustav Frielinghaus of II./JG 3, who recorded his 73rd and 74th victories, and Fw Horst Schlick of 1./JG 77, credited with his 27th and 28th.

RECORD-BREAKING OPERATION

The Salerno landings, which commenced on 3 September 1943, signalled the end of Axis hopes for offensive operations in the Mediterranean. Fascist Italy capitulated to the Allies five days later. There was very little in the way of resources available to the Luftwaffe for bombing operations south of central Italy, which meant that sporadic German attempts at local offensives in the eastern Mediterranean at the end of 1943 lacked sufficient air power to secure their success.

With the end of formal Italian resistance many garrisons in the Aegean Sea rose up against the Axis presence in the region. British forces were alerted to take this opportunity to sweep German forces away from the south of Greece but, with typical efficiency, enemy reinforcements were moved in to recapture some of the Dodecanese islands that had been hastily occupied by the Allies. There was little in the way of local British air power to challenge the initial German response, and the island of Rhodes became the primary Luftwaffe redoubt to counter the Royal Navy's attempts at controlling the seas. Three Stuka units were either based on Rhodes or used it as a staging post for attacks on Allied warships – several vessels were heavily damaged and had to be evacuated in the early part of October.

2Lt Harry Hanna was photographed alongside aircraft number '66' at around the time he claimed five kills on 9 October 1943 to 'make ace' (*Blake*)

To counter the air power imbalance that now left the Royal Navy vulnerable to Luftwaffe dive-bombers, P-38s of the 37th FS, commanded by Maj William Leverette, were temporarily moved from Algeria to Gambut, in Libya. Once again the remarkable combat range of the P-38 would prove invaluable to the Allies.

Lightnings from both the 1st and 14th FGs had landed at Gambut by 4 October. Aircraft from the 1st made it down in good order, but the P-38s of the 37th FS landed in virtual pitch darkness and nearly came to grief at the edge of a precipice, before being safely parked. Patrols over the vulnerable British ships began the next day, by which time Luftwaffe bombing attacks had already damaged several ships. And on 8 October the sloop HMS *Peacock* was crippled by bombs.

The next day a formation of British and Greek ships was attacked in the Scarpento Channel in the Aegean Sea southwest of Rhodes by II./StG 3's Ju 87s. The Rhodes-based Stuka unit sent its entire force of 26 dive-bombers against the Allied vessels, and they duly sank the destroyer HMS *Panther* and so badly damaged the cruiser HMS *Carlisle* that it would never put to sea again.

The attack was at its height when Maj Leverette arrived with seven P-38s from the 37th FS. Leaving three fighters to provide the unit with top cover, he swept down to attack the Stukas with the remaining four Lightnings. Leverette's combat report, written the next day, gives a contemporary view of the action;

'On 9 October 1943 our squadron took off at 1030 hrs with nine planes to cover a convoy of one cruiser and four destroyers. Two planes were forced to return because of engine trouble shortly after takeoff, leaving seven planes – a four-ship flight led by the undersigned and a three-ship flight led by Lt Blue. We sighted the convoy at 1200 hrs approximately 15 miles east of Cape Valoca, on the island of Scarpanto. The convoy had been attacked and the cruiser was smoking from the stern.

'During our first orbit around the convoy, while flying a southwesterly course at 8000 ft, Lt Sprinkle called out, "Bogies at one o'clock, slightly

Maj Bill Leverette, CO of the 37th FS/ 14th FG, stands beneath the newly-marked nose of his P-38H *Stingaree*. He is holding the propeller blade that was damaged in a collision with a Ju 87 during the record-breaking mission of 9 October 1943 (*Bill Leverette*)

high, approaching the convoy from the northwest". We immediately changed course to pass behind the bogies and began a gradual climb. Shortly thereafter, we identified the bogies as Ju 87s in three flights, totalling approximately 25. Lt Blue implicitly followed instructions to maintain his flight of three planes at altitude to cover my flight as we attacked the Ju 87s at about 1215 hrs.

'My flight immediately dived to the left and attacked the Ju 87s from the left quarter. I attacked an enemy aircraft in the rear of the formation, firing at about 20 degrees and observing smoke pouring from the left side of engine. I broke away to the left and upward, attacking a second enemy aircraft from the rear and slightly below. After a short burst at about 200 yards this enemy aircraft rolled over and spiralled steeply downwards. After breaking away to the left again and turning back towards the formation of Ju 87s, I saw both enemy aircraft strike the water. Apparently neither rear gunner fired at me.

'I attacked another enemy aircraft at a slight angle from the left rear, firing just after the rear gunner opened fire. He ceased firing immediately and the pilot jumped out, although I did not see the 'chute open.

'I continued into the formation and attacked another enemy aircraft from 30 degrees, observing cannon and machine gun hits in its engine. Large pieces of cowling and parts flew off and the engine immediately began smoking profusely as the enemy aircraft started down. Breaking away and upward to the left, I re-entered the formation and opened fire with cannon and machine guns on another Ju 87 from approximately 15 degrees. The canopy and parts flew off, a long flame immediately shot out from the rear of the engine and left wing root and the rear gunner jumped clear of the enemy aircraft.

'Continuing into the formation and attacking another enemy aircraft from a slight angle to the left rear and below, I was forced to roll partially on my back to the left to bring my sight onto the enemy aircraft, opening fire at close range. I observed full hits on the right upper side of the engine, which immediately began to smoke. I broke away slightly to the left, and my element leader, Lt Hanna, saw the Ju 87 strike the water. Attacking another aircraft from behind and slightly below, the rear gunner ceased firing after I hit him with a short burst. The enemy aircraft nosed downwards slightly and I closed to minimum range, setting the engine on fire with a full burst in the bottom of the fuselage. The enemy aircraft dived and I was unable to break away upwards. In attempting to pass under the right wing of the aircraft, three feet of my left propeller sliced through the enemy aircraft.

'We engaged the Ju 87s until they passed over the south coast of Rhodes at approximately 1230 hrs.'

The 37th FS's final victory tally for this mission was 16 Ju 87s destroyed. A lone Ju 88 that had strayed into the area was also despatched. All the P-38s returned safely home. Leverette's claim of seven kills in one engagement was the highest made by a USAAF pilot in Europe during the entire war. German records indicate that 11./StG 3 lost seven Ju 87s over the water and two more written off in crash-landings on Rhodes. Undoubtedly others were damaged and repaired. Despite the discrepancy in claims versus actual losses, there was no denying that the combat effectiveness of 11./StG 3 had been seriously affected when at least nine of its 26 dive-bombers were put out of action.

As an interesting footnote to this engagement, one of the Stukas was caught in the net of a fishing boat a few miles off the coast of Rhodes in 2004. Two years later the Royal Hellenic Air Force raised the wreckage and found that it was probably Ju 87D Wk-nr 100375 ('S7+GM') flown by Ltn Rolf Metzger and gunner Uffz Hans Sopnemann, both of whom were listed as missing in action. The wreckage was taken to the Royal Hellenic Air Force museum for restoration.

Maj Bill Leverette and 2Lt Harry Hanna had become the Twelfth Air Force's latest P-38 aces following this one-sided clash. As it happened, there would be few additional Lightning victories for pilots of the Twelfth Air Force because the new strategic Fifteenth Air Force would absorb all three P-38 groups, as well as the P-47-equipped 325th FG, upon its formation on 1 November 1943. That same day the new air force's first bombing mission was undertaken when a railway bridge in the province of La Spezia, in northeastern Italy, was attacked, followed by a heavy attack on industrial targets in the Austrian city of Wiener Neustadt the next day.

One of the few fighter pilots with kills that bridged the Twelfth and Fifteenth air forces, Maj Bill Leverette would file one more claim in 1943 when he reported downing a Bf 109 northeast of Eleusis airfield, in Greece, on 14 December. He would go on to claim an additional two Bf 110s and another Bf 109 in early 1944 to take his final score to 11 aerial victory claims.

Throughout the North African campaign, as well as the invasions of Sicily and Italy, P-38 units had fought mainly against the odds to make the twin-boom Lightning the predominant US fighter type in the Mediterranean theatre. By the end of 1943, 37 P-38 pilots had 'made ace', while 12 others had achieved the same distinction while flying Spitfires in the MTO.

There would be further honours for the P-38 in the Mediterranean theatre. 1Lt Bill 'Dixie' Sloan would remain its top-scoring ace until his tally of 12 was finally passed by the 325th FG's Maj Herschel Green on 7 April 1944 – almost nine months after Sloan had claimed his final kill. And the 82nd FG held high honours for the number of aircraft shot down in the MTO until its total was surpassed by the 31st FG in March 1945.

1Lt 'Dixie' Sloan of the 96th FS/82nd FG poses with his P-38G-5 42-12835 near the end of his combat tour in August, having accounted for eight German and four Italian aircraft between 7 January and 22 July 1943. He remained the top American ace in the Mediterranean until April 1944

THE MIGHTY EIGHTH

Northwestern Europe was the final theatre to which the P-38 was committed after the type's re-introduction to units within the Eighth and Ninth Air Forces during the second half of 1943. Irony abounds in the story of the Lightning's return to action from English bases. If it had enjoyed the same level of success reported in other theatres it would undoubtedly have been the premier American fighter type of the war. Then again, if P-38s had not been committed to the USAAF's resource-sapping daylight bombing offensive from Britain there might have been enough aircraft available for the Lightning to have had a decisive influence on the outcome of the conflict in the Pacific, the Mediterranean and the CBI.

The fact remained, however, that the European theatre took priority. Indeed, more P-38 units were deployed in England than anywhere else. There were seven P-38 groups in the Eighth and Ninth Air Forces compared with five in the Pacific, three in the Mediterranean and one in the CBI. While Mediterranean units were making do with G-models for most of 1943, the Eighth Air Force was assigned the P-38H and then took the lion's share of the much-improved J-models until the Lightning was phased out just after the Normandy landings in June 1944.

Yet for much of 1943 there were no P-38 fighters in England, as the last examples had been shipped to North Africa in January as attrition replacements for the Twelfth Air Force. The obvious need for long-range escort types after Eighth Air Force heavy bomber losses had become unsustainable in the middle of the year made USAAF planners consider the P-38 as an immediate solution to this pressing problem. One answer was to transfer the three P-38 groups from the Mediterranean back to England after North Africa had been secured by the Allies in May 1943. But vigorous objections by theatre commanders and the aircrafts' requirement by the nascent, strategic, Fifteenth Air Force prevailed, convincing Eighth Air Force planners to look elsewhere.

Two P-38 groups were duly found in California and Washington state, where they had been stripped of aircraft and personnel in early 1943 to meet the needs of the Mediterranean and Pacific theatres. However, the 20th and 55th FGs had laboured diligently during the early summer to return to strength, and they had reached operational status by August.

The 20th began its departure from March Field (later March Air Force Base, and headquarters of the Fifteenth Air Force in the postwar Strategic Air Command), California, on 11 August. The unit sailed on the *Queen Elizabeth* from New York City, finding itself in Scotland on the 25th and the uncompleted King's Cliffe airfield, in Northamptonshire, a few days later. The group immediately began preparing for operations.

Meanwhile, the 55th FG was also working up to operational status, but in the challenging conditions of the mountainous and cloudy Washington state. The group's personnel arrived in Scotland on 15 September and travelled to their new base of Nuthampstead, in Hertfordshire, the next day. Like King's Cliffe, Nuthampstead was a muddy airfield that required a good deal of hard work to bring it up to operational standards.

Some of its successful pilots found themselves sharing the hastily erected Nissen huts. 2Lts Bob Buttke (who subsequently became the 55th FG's second highest-scoring ace), Gene Fair (Buttke's wingman on some of his first successful missions), Jim Hiner and Hal Bauer were all in the same hut.

In a relatively short time the group became operational, but not soon enough to influence the outcome of the disastrous 14 October 1943 attack on Schweinfurt, which cost the USAAF 60 heavy bombers. The newly arrived fighter group might not have been much help even if it had been operational, since most new Eighth Air Force groups went through a 'seasoning period' in which painful lessons had to be absorbed before the unit could be expected to make a difference in combat.

As it happened, the 55th FG began its operational career the day after Schweinfurt. Led by group commander Col Frank James, 36 P-38s took off on the afternoon of 15 October on a two-hour sweep over the Dutch coast. They saw little of the enemy except for a few flak bursts. James was a P-38 enthusiast who took exception to criticism of its performance against single-engined Luftwaffe fighters. 'I'll stack my fighter against any other in the air', was his usual response. The first inconclusive clash between P-38s of the 55th and the Luftwaffe came on 23 October when several flights from the 343rd FS that were escorting B-26s over France at 12,000 ft were forced into extensive turning manoeuvres to shake off aggressive Fw 190s. 2Lts Jerry Brown (the first Eighth Air Force P-38 ace in mid-April 1944) and Don Penn were astounded to find Luftwaffe fighters on their tails for the first time. They were obliged to weave to protect each other all the way across the channel.

Success was finally achieved by the 55th over northern Europe on 3 November when the group escorted B-17s to Wilhelmshaven at about 30,000 ft – the target distance of about 530 miles was easily covered by P-38s fitted with external fuel tanks. JG 1 sent up a mixed force of Fw 190s and Bf 109s that was surprised to find American escorts this far into Germany. Of the 13 Luftwaffe fighters reported lost, six were attributed to P-47 pilots and, quite possibly, a few to B-17 gunners. The 55th's pilots claimed to have destroyed six and damaged a seventh, but they were credited with three confirmed and four probables. 2Lt Bob Buttke of the 343rd FS achieved his first two of five victories when he was credited with two Bf 109s during this mission.

Two days later this success was repeated during a B-24 escort mission to Münster. The 55th FG's 38th FS managed to stay with the bombers until Do 217 twin-engined fighters arrived and appeared to launch mortar shells or rockets at the bombers. Three of their escorting Bf 109s from JG 1 were reported to

Future P-38 ace 2Lt Bob Buttke of the 343rd FS/55th FG claimed two Bf 109Gs destroyed during his first combat on 3 November 1943

Three P-38H-5s of the 338th FS/ 55th FG were photographed at Nuthampstead in October 1943. Note the 165-gal external tanks on racks around the Tarmac. They gave the Lightning a major increase in range on missions over Occupied Europe (*Blake*)

have been shot down by the P-38s, including one by 1Lt Mark Shipman. Counting his successes in North Africa, this raised Shipman's score to three. Once again bomber losses were negligible.

From the time the P-38s returned to England in September until their first operation on 15 October, the Eighth Air Force had lost more than 250 bombers. After the Lightnings resumed operations there were just over 80 reported bomber losses due to enemy action over Europe in November. According to Lt Col Wesley Craven and Maj James Cates in their study of the US Army Air Force in World War 2, the immediate effect of the reintroduction of the P-38 to missions flown by the Eighth Air Force was a reduction of bomber losses to a supportable level.

Yet the limitations of performance and numbers attributed to the P-38 in Europe started to emerge as early as 7 November. A mission to escort Ninth Air Force B-26s raiding Meulan airfield in Normandy gave the 20th FG's 79th FS its combat debut, the unit accompanying the 55th FG so as to gain operational experience. Two Fw 190s dived through the bomber formation and attacked Capt Herbert Cumming, setting the right engine of his P-38 on fire. He was escorted back over the channel, but had to bail out and was lost in the frigid and choppy water. Maj John Wilkins was also lost when he took off ten minutes after the rest of the 79th and was never seen again. It was an unfortunate start for the 20th FG.

It was 55th FG's turn to endure a mauling by the Jagdwaffe less than a week later, the group fighting its first full-scale battle on 13 November during another escort mission to Bremen. Three Fw 190s, two Ju 88s, a Bf 109 and what was probably a Me 410 were claimed to have been shot down, but no fewer than five P-38s were definitely lost to German fighters and two others to unknown causes. Sixteen more Lightnings returned to base suffering varying degrees of battle damage. One of them was the aircraft flown by future 38th FS ace 2Lt Jerry Brown, which caused groundcrew at Nuthampstead to shake their heads in wonder that the aircraft had ever made it back at all. Brown had been flying as a member of Capt Joe Myers' flight about ten miles southwest of Bremen at 29,000 ft when determined German attacks split up the P-38s. Myers managed not only to protect the bombers but also to come to the rescue of his wingman. The engagement was described in his post-action report;

'We observed a Ju 88 approaching the middle box of bombers from the four o'clock position and at the bombers' level of 26,000 ft. We immediately initiated an attack upon him from above and behind. He observed our attack, fired his rockets and dived away to the right. I closed to within 500 yards, fired about a six-second burst and observed his right engine smoking violently. We were losing altitude rapidly, so I broke off the attack and pulled up into a spiralling zoom. As I did so, I observed an Me 109 on my wingman's tail

Maj Mark Shipman scored an early victory for the 38th FS/55th FG when he claimed a Bf 109 on 5 November 1943, possibly while flying this aircraft (P-38H-5 42-67080). *SKYLARK IV* was lost with its pilot, 2Lt Herbert T Winter, on 5 January 1944 (*Frank Birciel via Little Friends*)

38th FS/55th FG pilot 2Lt Jerry Brown was lucky to survive the group's first full-scale battle on 13 November 1943, returning to base with his P-38 badly shot up. He went on to become the 55th's first ace, claiming five victories in the Lightning between January and April 1944

about 50 yards behind him. I called him on the R/T, warning him to skid until I could position myself for an attack.

'Lt Brown took violent evasive action, doing dives, zooms, skids, rolls and various other manoeuvres, but the German continued to follow about 50 yards behind him, firing constantly. In the meantime I moved to a position about 150 yards behind him. I'd already fired about three or four large deflection shots of about one or two seconds' duration at the German but without any noticeable results. Finally, Lt Brown

Capt Chet Patterson was another leading light of the 55th FG, accounting for four German fighters before he completed his tour in the spring of 1944. He too had been successful during the fierce aerial battles fought in November 1943 (*Walter Konantz via Little Friends*)

tried a skidding barrel roll, but the Me 109 followed and put a long burst into Lt Brown's right engine, causing heavy brown smoke to pour out. At about the same time I had closed to within approximately 150 yards of the German, and followed them both into the roll. As the German fired at Lt Brown, I fired about a five-second burst with no deflection from an inverted position into the Me 109. His engine burst into flame and pieces of the plane flew all over the sky. I passed within 40 or 50 ft of him and observed fire from the engine streaming back over the fuselage. Lt Brown feathered his right engine and was able to make it to our home base.'

By the end of 1943 Joe Myers had three Bf 109s to his credit, and he would transfer to the P-47-equipped 78th FG in August 1944 and claim another Bf 109 and a share in a Me 262 for 4.5 aerial victories. With the addition of four confirmed strafing victories Myers would become an Eighth Air Force ace with a total of 8.5 claims.

November would not be an entirely grim month for the Eighth Air Force's P-38 units, however. For example, on 25 November the 55th FG's 338th FS claimed four Fw 190s from II./JG 26 destroyed for the loss of a P-38 during a sweep over the Lille area of France. The unit, led by Capt Chet Patterson, had used the P-38's manoeuvring flaps to good advantage to pounce on several flights of German fighters. One of the Fw 190s confirmed as destroyed was attributed to Patterson. Three more were probably destroyed and two damaged. One of the Fw 190s claimed destroyed had been flown by Luftwaffe *experte* Maj Johannes Siefert, *Gruppenkommandeur* of II./JG 26 and victor over 57 Allied aircraft. He had collided with the fighter flown by 338th FS pilot 2Lt Manuel Aldecoa. Both pilots perished.

The next day there was yet another trip to Bremen, and this time eight P-38s from the 20th FG's 77th FS went along with the 55th FG to gain operational experience. Maj Herbert Johnson was leading the 20th FG formation, and he managed to get within range of one of five Do 217s that were probably trying to break up the bomber formation with rockets. Johnson, who had only been assigned to the 20th since 13 November, made the most of the opportunity when he got to within 200 yards of the aircraft before opening fire. Seeing his bullets hit the enemy aircraft around its cockpit, Johnson observed balls of flame shoot back from the Dornier before it spun away. Johnson was another P-38 pilot who just missed becoming an Eighth Air Force ace, claiming three fighters in the air and another on the ground before ending his tour in August 1944 and returning home.

HARD LESSONS LEARNED

By December 1943 the Eighth Air Force's P-38 veterans had already learned the bitter lessons of operating their Lightnings in the hostile skies of northern Europe. The advantages apparent in other theatres such as speed, range and firepower were still valid in the ETO, but the cold conditions of high altitude operations revealed other factors that demanded new tactics.

For example, pilots operating from England quickly learned that the P-38's power-to-weight ratio deteriorated above 24,000 ft. Conditions in-theatre demanded that escort fighters often operated above 30,000 ft, and that revealed unfortunate traits in the P-38. Capt Don Penn confided to the author some 30 years after the war that a useful tactic when an engagement was imminent was to descend to 24,000 ft and turn to face any pursuing Luftwaffe fighters. Penn insisted that when the P-38 formation reached 24,000 ft 'everything would be just fine' in combat with German aircraft.

A tactic that particularly annoyed 55th FG pilots was the practice of having an entire P-38 squadron following and protecting the leader, who would invariably miss his shot at an escaping Luftwaffe fighter which meant that the guns of up to 15 P-38s trailing behind him could not be brought to bear. Capt Chet Patterson successfully defied this tactic when he ordered his flights to fight individually, enabling every gun to fire at the enemy. Patterson had a confirmed score of four single-engined Luftwaffe fighters to his credit by the end of his tour, and it is believed that his flight consistently returned to base without losing a man.

The group's pilots were also frustrated when visiting Eighth Air Force commanders failed to consult them about the effectiveness of P-38 operations. As a result, it was the same group leaders who promoted ineffective battle tactics and then blamed the fighter for the 55th FG's less than impressive combat record. Uninspired leadership at group level was, therefore, partly to blame for the Lightning's poor reputation as a fighter in the ETO.

An Eighth Air Force veteran explained that it was possible for a P-38 flight being pursued by the Luftwaffe to turn the tables by using the Lightning's intrinsic manoeuvrability and superior climb performance. By splitting the flight into climbing turns in opposite directions, the pursuing German fighters would be presented with a difficult choice. If they followed one group of P-38s the other one would be in an attacking position before the pursuing Luftwaffe aircraft could press home their advantage. A wise German pilot would break off contact by making a split-S manoeuvre and dive away.

Seven P-38s were lost over the cold European battleground during December. The destruction of no more than five Luftwaffe aircraft in return brought a sober end to the 55th FG's first two months of combat. One notable victory was achieved on 13 December when 343rd FS pilots 1Lts Bob Buttke and Jim Hiner encountered a Ju 88 during a 490-mile escort mission to Kiel, on Germany's North Sea coast. Both pilots attacked the aircraft and it was seen to fall in flames, with at least one crewman parachuting to safety before it crashed. Buttke and Hiner fired at about the same time, but only Hiner received credit for the enemy aircraft's destruction.

Capt Don Penn was a 55th FG stalwart during the group's time with the Eighth Air Force. He claimed one aerial victory while flying the P-38, as well as an Me 262 after the group had switched to the P-51D. His opinion of the Lightning's qualities as a fighter was higher than that of his group's leadership (*Penn*)

Three more Luftwaffe fighters were claimed by the 55th on the last day of the year during an escort mission to Bordeaux. Capt Joe Myers, who was flying a brand new P-38J-10, got his third confirmed Bf 109 two miles north of Blaye-et-Sainte-Luce.

Officially, there were no victories yet for the 20th FG, other than the one credited to Maj Herbert Johnson while the 79th FS was attached to the 55th FG. However, one of the squadron's most successful pilots who would become a P-38 ace in February 1944 did make his first mark in aerial combat on 31 December 1943. 1Lt Lindol Graham claimed to have damaged an Fw 190 over Bordeaux – an event he described in his combat report;

'I was leading the 79th FS, flying lead ship in White Flight. We were sweeping the target area, slightly south and west of the target, at 22,000 ft. I saw two Fw 190s below just as the group leader reported them. I peeled off with my flight and started down, keeping my belly tanks because I wanted the gas in case of a fight on the way home. I used 50 inches [of boost] and 2650 rpm to gain speed in the dive. My wingman was Flt Off Byrd, and he was following me down.

'The Fw 190 was in a gentle turn as I approached from 45 degrees. In order to pull out and follow him I used combat flaps to help me come out of my dive. The plane came out of the dive very nicely, even with belly tanks, at an indicated airspeed of over 375 mph. I followed the Fw 190, and at about 350 yards and an angle of about ten degrees I opened fire with four .50-cals. I was closing slowly and saw four or five hits on his right wing just before he went into the overcast. I pulled up and started climbing back up from 10,000 ft.

'My second element stayed about 3000 ft over me during the engagement, and another flight stayed at 20,000 ft. My wingman and the rest of the flight provided protection during the whole engagement.'

During tests with captured Fw 190s it was found that the P-38 would have its best chance of victory between 22,000 ft and 24,000 ft. The Fw 190 displayed superior acceleration and turning radius at lower altitudes and eventually outstripped the P-38 in power ratings at other altitudes. After June 1944 the disadvantage suffered by the P-38 in the rolling plane and in a dive were largely remedied by the power-assisted ailerons and dive brakes of the P-38J-25. That aircraft, however, was issued exclusively to groups in the Ninth Air Force.

These three P-38H-5s of the 338th FS/55th FG were flown from their Nuthampstead base to the 91st BG's airfield at Bassingbourn, in Cambridgeshire, on 12 December 1943

APPENDICES

Early P-38 Lightning Aces

(At 31 December 1943 – final P-38 score and fate, if killed/captured in 1943, in brackets)

South and Southwest Pacific Theatres

Richard Bong	21 (40)
Thomas McGuire	16 (38)
Edward Cragg	15 (15) (KIA 26/12/43)
Tom Lynch	13 (17)
Jay Robbins	13 (22)
Danny Roberts	12 (12) (KIA 9/11/43)
Murray Shubin	11 (11)
Ken Sparks	11 (11)
James Watkins	11 (11)
Bill Harris	10 (16)
Paul Stanch	10 (10)
Grover Fanning	9 (9)
Gerald Johnson	9 (20)
Frank Lent	9 (11)
George Welch	9 (9)
David Allen	8 (8)
Fred Harris	8 (8)
John Jones	8 (8)
Charles MacDonald	8 (27)
John O'Neill	8 (8)
Zach Dean	7 (7)
Vincent Elliott	7 (7)
Kenneth Ladd	7 (12)
John Loisel	7 (11)
Cornelius Smith	7 (11)
Richard Smith	7 (7)
Robert Westbrook	7 (13)
Stanley Andrews	6 (6)
Edward Czarnecki	6 (6)
Edwin DeGraffenreid	6 (6)
Hoyt Eason	6 (6) (KIA 8/3/43)
Charles Gallup	6 (6)
James Ince	6 (6)
John Lane	6 (6)
Thomas Lanphier	6 (6)
John Smith	6 (6) (KIA 9/11/43)
Elliott Summer	6 (10)
Robert Adams	5 (5) (KIA 2/9/43)
Harry Brown	5 (5)
Vivian Cloud	5 (5)
Billy Gresham	5 (6)
Allen Hill	5 (9)
Besby Holmes	5 (5)
Charles King	5 (5)
Marion Kirby	5 (5)
Lowell Lutton	5 (5) (KIA 2/11/43)
Jack Mankin	5 (5)
John Mitchell	5 (5)
Jennings Myers	5 (5) (KIA 22/12/43)
Ralph Wandrey	5 (5)
Arthur Wenige	5 (5)

Mediterranean Theatre

William Sloan	12 (12)
Frank Hurlbut	9 (9)
Louis Curdes	8 (8)
William Leverette	8 (11)
Charles Zubarik	8 (8) (PoW 24/5/43)
Claude Kinsey	7 (7) (PoW 5/4/43)
Ward Kuentzel	7 (7)
Lawrence Liebers	7 (7)
Herbert Ross	7 (7)
Meldrum Sears	7 (7)
Harley Vaughn	7 (7)
Edward Waters	7 (7)
Richard Campbell	6 (6)
Ray Crawford	6 (6)
John Mackay	6 (6)
William Schildt	6 (6)
Virgil Smith	6 (6) (KIA 30/12/42)
Thomas White	6 (6)
Jack Ilfrey	5.5 (7.5)
Leslie Andersen	5 (5)
Paul Cochran	5 (5)
Rodney Fisher	5 (5)
Harry Hanna	5 (5)
Daniel Kennedy	5 (5)
Carroll Knott	5 (5)
Marlow Leikness	5 (5)
T H McArthur	5 (5) (KIFA 3/5/43)
Ernest Osher	5 (5)
Joel Owens	5 (5)
Newell Roberts	5 (5)
Gerald Rounds	5 (5)
Herman Visscher	5 (5)
Sidney Weatherford	5 (5)
Darrell Welch	5 (5)
Lee Wiseman	5 (5)
John Wolford	5 (5) (KIA 19/5/43)

1

P-38E 41-2076 *ITSY BITSY* of Capt George Laven Jr, 54th FS/343rd FG, Fort Glenn airfield, Aleutian Islands, October 1942

Laven joined the 54th FS in the late summer of 1942 and was assigned this early-model Lightning. He flew it until the end of the year, even though the P-38E had been put on the restricted list due to its obsolescence in October 1942. Laven was ordered to fly the fighter from Fort Glenn, on Umnak Island, to an Alaskan repair depot in November 1942, and he was frustrated to find the facility closed when he arrived. He took the unorthodox step of pressing on to an open facility near his home in San Antonio, Texas! After the P-38 was repaired – and Laven had visited his family – he simply flew back into the war. He is credited with a share in the destruction on the sea of a 'Mavis' flying boat during a long-range mission on 3 September 1942, and with also shooting down two Zero-sens on 13 February 1943. Laven was also credited with an 'Emily' flying boat, which he shot down whilst at the controls of a 49th FG P-38L late in the Pacific War.

2

P-38F-5 42-12621 of Capt Curran L Jones, 39th FS/35th FG, Port Moresby, New Guinea, November 1942

Jones scored his first victory while flying a P-39 in June 1942 and opened his account as a P-38 pilot with two Ki-43 'Oscars' claimed destroyed and another probably destroyed over the Lae convoy on 6 January 1943. He probably destroyed a Zero-sen over the Bismarck Sea convoy on 2 March 1943 and claimed two more during the following day's battle. All of Jones' Lightning claims came in this particular aircraft.

3

P-38F (serial unknown) of Capt Robert L Faurot, 39th FS/35th FG, Port Moresby, New Guinea, November 1942

This aircraft was possibly the fighter flown by Faurot when he was posted on detached duty to Guadalcanal in November 1942, and it was probably the fighter he was using when he made his remarkable claim of downing a Zero-sen with a bomb that same month. He also claimed to have shot down an 'Oscar' over a Japanese convoy on 8 January 1943 for his only other confirmed victory. Maj Gen George Kenney cited a highly dubious report that Faurot had accounted for other Japanese fighters during the Bismarck Sea battle on 3 March 1943 in which he was killed.

4

P-38F-1 41-7649 *"WALLY"* of Capt Wade C Walles, CO of the 48th FS/14th FG, Tafaroui, Algeria, December 1942

Walles spent many hours in the cockpit of this aircraft, flying it across the Atlantic from Labrador to Greenland and then from Iceland to Scotland. In November 1942 he flew it to North Africa to participate in Operation *Torch*. Walles endured a difficult, abbreviated, tour during which he claimed the destruction of a Bf 110 shared with another pilot on 4 December. Two days later he claimed a Ju 52/3m and, finally, a Bf 109 on 30 December. The two vertical red stripes on the fighter's twin booms signified that this aircraft belonged to the squadron CO, and that it was part of A Flight.

5

P-38F-5 42-12627 *Loi* of 1Lt Charles S Gallup, 39th FS/35th FG, Port Moresby, New Guinea, January 1943

Gallup used this P-38F-5 to down a 'Zeke' on 27 December 1942 for his first victory claim. However, he 'made ace' at the controls of Capt Jones' 42-12621. Having downed a pair of 'Oscars', with another claimed as probably destroyed, on 7 January 1943, Gallup was credited with two more Ki-43s destroyed and another as a 'probable' over the Lae-bound convoy the following day.

6

P-38G-13 43-2338 *Phoebe* of Capt Thomas G Lanphier, 339th FS/347th FG, Guadalcanal, Solomon Islands, April 1943

Lanphier scored the first victory for the 70th FS on 24 December 1942, his Zero-sen kill being the only success achieved by the unit that day. It apparently appears in error on some lists as a P-39K claim as the 70th was operating the Bell fighter alongside the P-38 at the time. Lanphier, however, was flying a Lightning. Integrated into the 339th FS on Guadalcanal in March 1943 when the unit converted from P-39s to P-38s, he was credited with downing three 'Zekes' on 7 April towards the end of Operation *I-Go*. Finally, Lanphier was flying *Phoebe* during Operation *Vengeance* – the interception of Adm Yamamoto – on 18 April, during which he claimed to have downed a 'Betty' bomber as well as one of the escorting 'Zekes'. Post-war research, however, reveals that Lanphier shared the destruction of Yamamoto's aircraft and uncovered the fact that no Zero-sens were listed in Japanese accounts as being lost. Lanphier was perhaps over-enthusiastic in his claims. Indeed, on one occasion he reported shooting down a Zero-sen while manning a gunner's position in the B-17 in which he was flying as a passenger.

7

P-38G-13 43-2187 *Diablo* of 1Lt Rex T Barber, 339th FS/347th FG, Guadalcanal, Solomon Islands, April 1943

Barber gained an aerial victory while flying a P-39D with the 70th FS on 28 December 1942 – an achievement of which he was extremely proud. Subsequently integrated into the 339th FS, he probably scored his first P-38 victories in *Diablo* on 7 April 1943 when he was credited with destroying two Zero-sens over Cape Esperance. As with Tom Lanphier, Barber's achievements during *Vengeance* are somewhat obscure. He undoubtedly played a major role in the destruction of both Japanese bombers at the centre of the operation. Indeed, some researchers credit him with shooting down both 'Bettys'. The fact that Japanese accounts reveal the loss of no escorting Zero-sens further confuses the situation surrounding the award of credits for no fewer than three IJNAF fighters destroyed, even though the claims remain intact. At one extreme, Barber is possibly the victor over three Japanese aircraft during the operation, but it is undoubtedly right that he should be credited with at least one-half of each bomber.

8

P-38F-1 (serial unknown) *Sky Ranger* of Capt Darrell G Welch, 27th FS/1st FG, Chateaudun-du-Rhumel, Algeria, April 1943

This fighter was probably the P-38 that Welch was flying when he left England with the 1st FG to participate in the *Torch* landings in North Africa in early November 1942. On 12 January

Welch damaged a Bf 109, and six days later he shot one down (and damaged a second) near Tripoli airfield. Another Messerschmitt fell to his guns on 23 March. Welch completed his scoring during an interception of German transport aircraft off Cap Bon on 5 April, when he claimed three Ju 52/3ms destroyed and another damaged. His tour was completed later in the month, and he probably flew the same P-38 throughout his combat career.

9
P-38G-13 43-2242 *Oriole* of 2Lt Murray J Shubin, 339th FS/ 347th FG, Guadalcanal, Solomon Islands, June 1943
This P-38 was almost certainly the one that Shubin was flying when he set a scoring record for the type by claiming five 'Zekes' destroyed and a sixth as a probable on 16 June 1943 over the Russell Islands. He already had a 'Rufe' floatplane fighter and a 'Zeke' to his credit by then. Shubin was flying a P-38H when he claimed his last four victories over the Solomons in October 1943.

10
P-38G-10 42-13415 *LITTLE BUTCH II* of 1Lt Thomas D Harmon, 'Squadron X', Lingling, China, July 1943
Harmon flew this P-38 from North Africa to China in 1942 with 'Squadron X', which eventually became the 449th FS of the 51st FG. The original *LITTLE BUTCH* had been a B-25 that Harmon had flown prior to him being transferred to the P-38. His only success as a fighter pilot in China came on 30 October 1943 when the 449th lost four Lightnings, including *LITTLE BUTCH II*, whilst claiming four Japanese aircraft destroyed. According to JAAF sources only one 'Oscar' was listed as missing following the engagement, however. Nevertheless, Harmon was credited with shooting down two before he was forced to abandon his fighter and face a harrowing 32-day trek back to Allied-held territory. Harmon is also noted for his associations with the entertainment world, including his film star wife Elyse Knox, after whom *LITTLE BUTCH* was named, and his actor son, Mark Harmon.

11
P-38G-15 43-2212 *RUFF STUFF* of Capt Norbert Ruff, 80th FS/ 8th FG, Port Moresby, New Guinea, July 1943
Ruff was a mainstay of the 80th FS from its P-39 days of mid-1942 until the end of 1943. He was credited with four confirmed victories while flying *RUFF STUFF*, starting with an 'Oscar' on 23 July 1943. He added two more Ki-43s near Dagua airstrip on 13 September and completed his scoring run with another 'Oscar' (or possibly a 'Hamp') two days later. Ruff was one of the 'old hands' of the 80th, and he passed on much of his experience to the younger pilots. He was reputed to have helped the last generation of squadron aces to sharpen their skills in battle.

12
P-38F-5 42-12653 of Capt Charles King, 39th FS/35th FG, Port Moresby, New Guinea, July 1943
This P-38 received special attention by the engineering-oriented aces Charlie King and Tom Lynch. The latter introduced innovations that gave the Lightning an edge in combat, and he was the first to install a bomb shackle camera that eliminated vibration-generated distortion from the nose camera mounted beneath the P-38 cannon. He also introduced some minor technical changes that made the fighter slightly faster and more responsive. As a result, the subject of this profile was routinely in demand by other 39th pilots for combat operations.

Dick Bong used it to score his fifth victory over the Lae convoy on 8 January 1943, while Hoyt Eason was flying this aircraft when he claimed to have shot down three Japanese fighters on 31 December 1942 to become the first P-38 ace of the Southwest Pacific area. King used 42-12653 to destroy one 'Oscar' and probably down another on 21 July 1943. They were the only claims he made while flying this aircraft.

13
P-38G-10 42-13437 *Golden Eagle* of 1Lt Robert Schultz, 449th FS/51st FG, Lingling, China, July 1943
Schultz flew this P-38 to China at the same time as Thomas Harmon flew his aircraft to the CBI theatre from North Africa. Between August 1943 and March 1944 Schultz shot down five enemy aircraft, claimed a sixth as a probable and damaged a seventh while flying this aircraft. 42-13437 remained in service after Schultz's tour expired in March 1944, the veteran fighter being assigned to 2Lt Jim Heitketter, who renamed it *Blacklace*.

14
P-38H-1 42-66532 *JAPANESE SANDMAN II* of 1Lt Richard E Smith, 39th FS/35th FG, Port Moresby, New Guinea, September 1943
Smith began flying with the 39th FS while the unit was being re-equipped with P-38s in late 1942. He achieved one of the squadron's first victories with the Lightning on 6 January 1943 when he claimed an 'Oscar' over the Lae convoy. He was also credited with some of the first successes over the Ki-61 'Tony' on 21 July 1943. Smith's sole victory in this aircraft was achieved over the Lae area on 22 September 1943 when he downed a 'Zeke' for his seventh, and last, kill.

15
P-38G (serial unknown) *Chicken Dit* of 1Lt Gerald L Rounds, 97th FS/82nd FG, Maddelina (Gerbini Satellite Field No 2), Sicily, September 1943
One of the original members of the 82nd FG in December 1942, Rounds remained a unit stalwart until his tour expired in September 1943. He scored his first victory, over a Bf 109, near Gabes on 11 February 1943, and claimed to have destroyed five Messerschmitts, plus one probably destroyed and two damaged, before his tour ended. Originally named *Cadiz Eagle*, this particular P-38G was flown by Rounds for much of his time with the group. Called *Chicken Dit* from early July, the fighter was used by Rounds to 'make ace' on 11 September when he downed a Bf 109 whilst covering the Salerno landings. The veteran fighter was shot up in the same action, however, losing its hydraulics and then being written off when Rounds had to belly land at the group's temporary Sicilian base at Maddelina.

16
P-38H-5 42-66820 of 1Lt Jay T Robbins, 80th FS/8th FG, Port Moresby, New Guinea, September 1943
Robbins gained his first three confirmed victories while flying P-38G-15 43-2382 on 21 July 1943. He was using 42-66820, however, when he made his next claims on 4 September, which elevated him to the status of ace. Robbins claimed four 'Zekes' destroyed in a battle over the Huon Gulf, and followed this feat up with a second four-victory haul (all 'Hamps') on 24 October over Rabaul – again in 42-66820. He may also have been flying this P-38 when he gained his final victories of 1943, downing two 'Zekes' over Cape Gloucester on 26 December. Robbins assumed command of the 80th FS after fellow high-scoring ace Maj Ed Cragg was killed in action on 26 December 1943.

17

P-38F-5 42-12659, *Lil' Woman 2nd* of 1Lt Stanley O Andrews, 39th FS/35th FG, Port Moresby, New Guinea, September 1943

One of the initial cadre of experienced P-38 pilots to reach New Guinea in late 1942, Andrews did much to prepare the 39th FS for combat in the Lockheed fighter. An unusual feature of his tour was that he used the same aircraft – 42-12659 – throughout his time on operations. He was credited with his first victory in it over Buna in December 1942 as well as his last in the Wewak area on 20 August 1943. At least two other victories were achieved by Andrews while flying this P-38, and all nine of his claims (six kills and three probables) were against Japanese fighters. The fact that an early model Lightning saw more than eight months of flying in the frontline is indicative of the low priority given to the Pacific theatre in comparison to the ETO before the D-Day landings.

18

P-38G-15 43-2203 of Capt George S Welch, 80th FS/8th FG, Port Moresby, New Guinea, September 1943

Welch was already an ace when he joined the 80th in the middle of 1943. He had claimed four Japanese aircraft while flying a P-40B of the 47th PS during the Pearl Harbor attack and three more exactly a year later in a P-39D with the 36th FS over the Buna area. P-38G-15 43-2203 was already an 80th FS veteran when Welch joined the squadron and was assigned this aircraft. He quickly built up his victory score while flying it, claiming two 'Zekes' (or 'Oscars') in the Lae area on 21 June. In August he claimed three 'Tonys' in P-38H-1 43-66578, before reverting to 43-2203 to complete an impressive combat career by claiming three 'Zekes' (more likely 'Oscars') and a Ki-46 'Dinah' on 2 September 1943. Welch ended his tour later in September and returned home to begin a distinguished test pilot career with North American Aviation in 1944. 43-2203 was lost over Rabaul on 2 November 1943, along with its pilot, Flt Off Willis Evers.

19

P-38H-1 42-66504 of 2Lt Zach W Dean, 432nd FS/475th FG, Dobodura, New Guinea, September 1943

Dean's first five confirmed claims were all made while he was flying this P-38. He had previously been awarded a probable while serving with his former unit, the 80th FS. Dean's first two claims as a Lightning pilot came during the invasion of Lae on 22 September 1943, when he destroyed a 'Betty' and a 'Zeke'. He later accounted for a 'Val' dive-bomber over Oro Bay on 15 October and became an ace nine days later when he shot down a 'Zeke' and a 'Hamp' over Rabaul. Always a fiery individual, Zach Dean accounted for his final two kills ('Zekes') while flying a P-38H-5 during the 22 December 1943 mission over Wewak.

20

P-38G-13 43-2204 *Beautiful Lass* of 2Lt John G O'Neill, 9th FS/49th FG, Dobodura, New Guinea, September 1943

John 'Jump' O'Neill had met Dick Bong during training when he looped the Golden Gate Bridge – a feat sometimes attributed to Bong. The two joined the 9th FS at about the same time, O'Neill scoring his first victory, over a Zero-sen, on 4 March 1943 – 24 hours after Bong had claimed his sixth. During an engagement on 28 March north of Oro Bay, O'Neill claimed a 'Hamp', but then went into a fallow period until he scored a run of six victories in October. His final four successes were gained over Rabaul almost certainly in 43-2204.

21

P-38G-15 (serial unknown) *Barney B* of 2Lt Harry T Hanna, 37th FS/14th FG, Gambut, Libya, October 1943

Hanna joined the 37th FS in June 1943, and operational rosters indicate that he had his first and only taste of aerial combat on 9 October over a Royal Navy convoy off the island of Rhodes. He completed the 50 missions of his tour in early 1944 and was eventually rotated home. His usual P-38 was marked with the squadron number '72', and he was flying it on 9 October when there was much confusion matching claims to actual German losses, which was not unusual. On this occasion the P-38 pilots counted the numerous splashes in the Aegean Sea below them as confirmed kills. Whatever the actual number of enemy aircraft lost, the fact remains that Hanna and his fellow P-38 pilots dealt the Ju 87 formation a heavy blow that must have significantly affected the morale of II./StG 3.

22

P-38H-1 42-66686 of 2Lt Henry Meigs, 12th FS/18th FG, Guadalcanal, Solomon Islands, October 1943

Gaining victories over three 'Betty' bombers in August and September 1943 while flying a modified P-38G of the 6th NFS in the early morning hours made Meigs one of the premier Lightning nightfighter pilots. He transferred to the 12th FS soon afterwards, and apparently flew this P-38H for the rest of the year. Having briefly served with the 417th NFS in December 1943, Meigs rejoined his very first unit (339th FS/347th FG) the following month and duly scored three more victories over the Rabaul area in daylight hours in February to 'make ace'.

23

P-38H-5 42-67004 *Haleakala* of 1Lt Harry Sealy, 459th FS/80th FG, Kurmitola, India, November 1943

'Lighthorse' Harry Sealy joined the 459th FS in October 1943 and received this P-38 the following month. He was apparently unable to claim the destruction of any enemy aircraft in the air or on the ground while flying the fighter. The fact that few operations were flown in late 1943 had probably prevented Sealy from enjoying success while flying his first Lightning. It was not until he received P-38H-5 42-66986 in March 1944 that he was able to achieve almost immediate success, claiming one 'Oscar' in the air and two Ki-21 'Sally' bombers on the ground in Burma on the 11th. In April Sealy used the same fighter to add further claims for two 'Oscars' shot down and three destroyed on the ground. By the end of May (now flying P-38J-5 42-67291) Sealy had 4.5 aerial claims and six strafing victories to his credit.

24

P-38G-15 43-2386 *'LIL-DE-ICER'/ 'G.I. ANNIE'* of 1Lt John L Jones, 80th FS/8th FG, Port Moresby, New Guinea, November 1943

43-2386 was one of the most distinguished P-38s in the Southwest Pacific, being used by various pilots including Jones, Cy Homer and Ken Ladd to gain at least 13 confirmed victories. Indeed, Jones claimed his first three kills with the fighter in May and July 1943, as did Homer – his victories came in August. Ladd claimed his second victory with the aircraft in September. The artwork on either side of the fighter's nose was based on publicity photographs of movie star Frances Rafferty. There seem to have been various artworks featured on the port side of the gun bay during the fighter's time with the 80th FS, although the only name recorded is *'LIL-DE-ICER'*. 43-2386 and its pilot, Flt Off Robert Gentile, were lost in bad weather over St George's Channel, near New Britain, on 7 November 1943.

25

P-38G-1 42-12705 *COTTON DUSTER/LILLY NELL* **of 1Lt Cyril F Homer, 80th FS/8th FG, Port Moresby, New Guinea, November 1943**

Homer was considered by some of his peers to be one of the theatre's best fighter pilots, even though he did not have a particularly high score. Nevertheless, he performed creditably when he engaged the enemy, achieving four victories in a single battle at least once. Homer 'made ace' in this particular aircraft when he downed an 'Oscar' over Dagua on 13 September 1943. He had despatched a 'Zeke' with it nine days earlier, and also used the fighter to make two probable claims on 7 November. He would go on to score ten more victories flying H-, J- and L-model Lightnings in 1944.

26

P-38H-5 42-67080 *SKYLARK IV* **of Maj Mark K Shipman, 38th FS/55th FG, Nuthampstead, England, November 1943**

Having already served a short but strenuous combat tour with the 48th FS/14th FG in North Africa, Shipman accepted another difficult assignment with the 55th FG. He duly became involved in the P-38's initial combat deployment over northern Europe, escorting American heavy bombers on prolonged deep penetration missions. Shipman already had two aerial claims to his credit, having shot down an Italian twin-engined aircraft on 22 November and a Me 323 six-engined transport on 15 January 1943. His sole victory with the 38th FS (which he led from 1 December 1943 through to 10 February 1944) was achieved over a Bf 109 on 5 November 1943, possibly while flying this aircraft.

27

P-38H-5 (serial number unknown) *Journey's End* **of Capt Joseph Myers, 38th FS/55th FG, Nuthampstead, England, November 1943**

For some unknown reason, Myers wanted the skull design displayed on his P-38 to be as gruesome as possible, and he instructed artist Sgt Bob Sand to paint blood dripping from its mouth. Sand was unhappy about this and the end result was a compromise, although it was still grim enough to be acceptable to Myers. He was probably flying this machine when he achieved his first aerial victory on 5 November 1943 on a day when his squadronmates, including Maj Shipman, filed claims for the destruction of five Bf 109s. Myers was credited with two more victories before the end of the year, the first of these also being claimed in *Journey's End* on 13 November – he downed another Bf 109 and damaged a Ju 88. The fighter was reportedly written off in an accident shortly thereafter. Myers, who claimed a further 1.5 kills while leading the P-47D-equipped 82nd FS/78th FG in 1944, survived the war with 4.5 aerial and four strafing victories to his name.

28

P-38H-1 42-66570 *VIRGIN/NULLI SECUNDUS* **of 1Lt Kenneth G Ladd, 80th FS/8th FG, Port Moresby, New Guinea, November 1943**

Ken Ladd was one of the most popular and reputedly one of the least skilful pilots in the 80th FS, so his score of 12 confirmed aerial claims is perhaps testament more to his daring and persistence than to his ability with the P-38. He achieved only one confirmed success while flying this P-38, downing an 'Oscar' in the Wewak area on 15 September, although he probably continued to use the aircraft until the end of the year – by which time his tally stood at seven victories. His first victory of 1944 was also claimed in a P-38H-1 (possibly this aircraft), Ladd downing a 'Zeke' over Wewak on 23 January.

29

P-38H-5 42-66826 *"Hold Everything"* **of 1Lt Paul V Morriss, 431st FS/475th FG Dobodura, New Guinea, December 1943**

This was the first P-38 assigned to future five-victory ace Paul Morriss, who joined the 475th FG in July 1943. He was flying it when he claimed to have shot down a 'Zeke' over Oro Bay on 15 October 1943. Apparently, Morriss used this fighter until well into December of that year, although he made his second claim (a 'Val' dive-bomber) over Cape Gloucester on 26 December, while flying an H-1. Morriss' last three victories (all 'Oscars') were scored in June 1944 in a P-38J.

30

P-38H-5 42-66742 *"The" WOFFLEDIGIT/FIFINELLA* **of Capt Verl E Jett, 431st FS/475th FG, Dobodura, New Guinea, December 1943**

This P-38 was flown by Capt Jett from the time he achieved his first P-38 victories, over a pair of 'Oscars' in the Wewak area on 18 August 1943, until at least the end of the year. He had assumed command of the 431st FS on 22 November 1943, and by the time his tour ended in April 1944 he had achieved one victory while flying P-39s with the 36th FS/8th FG and six others with the 475th FG. There is evidence to suggest that Jett flew this same P-38 throughout 1943, the fighter initially being named *Thoughts of Midnite*. This was later changed to *"The" WOFFLEDIGIT/FIFINELLA* when he assumed command of the squadron. The origin and meaning of *"The" Woffledigit* is obscure, but *Fifinella* was the creation of children's author Roald Dahl, who by then had already become an ace with the RAF. His book *Gremlins* featured troublesome creatures who played unsavoury tricks on the mechanical and fuel systems of aircraft. The female *Gremlins* were exactly the opposite in character, helping the pilot get through a mission without great difficulty.

INDEX